MAKE YOUR OWN
WORLD OF THE THEATRE

Extracts from the libretto of *La Bohème* by Giacomo Puccini by kind permission of Messrs G. Ricordi and Co.

ANGUS & ROBERTSON PUBLISHERS
London · Sydney · Melbourne

First published in the United Kingdom by Angus & Robertson (UK) Ltd 1982
First published in Australia by Angus & Robertson Publishers, Australia, 1982

Copyright © Rosemary Lowndes and Claude Kaïler 1982

Photography by Donald Southern

ISBN 0 207 14571 7

Typeset in Linotron 202 Univers and Bembo by Graphicraft Typesetters
Printed in Singapore

Make your own

writter

World of the Theatre

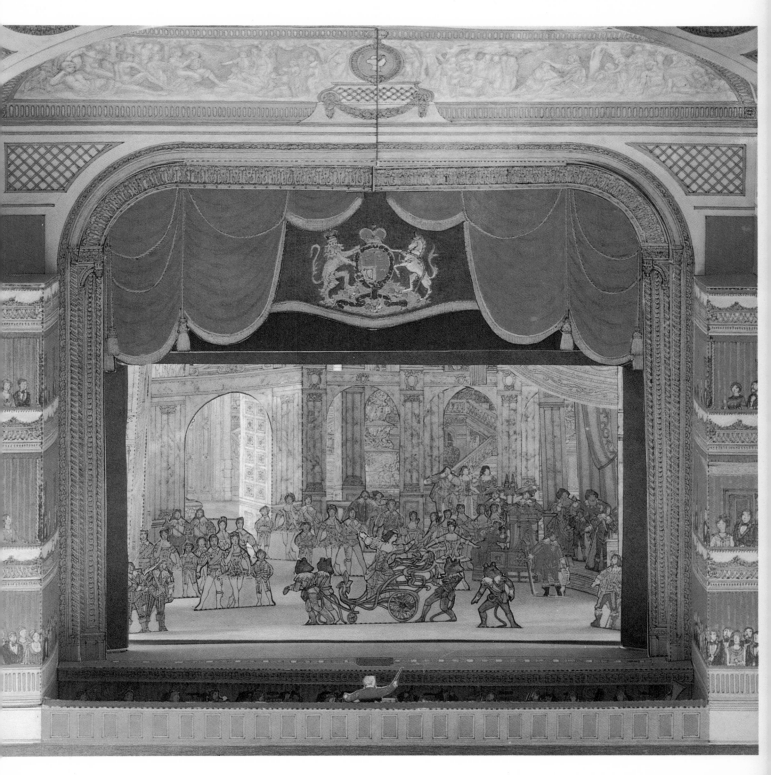

...and designed by Rosemary Lowndes and Claude Kailer

Angus & Robertson Publishers

My first reaction on seeing this lovely book was that I wished somebody had given it to me when I was younger — not only for the hours of enjoyment I would have had in constructing the stage and sets of this beautiful theatre, but for the marvellous insight it would have given me to the world I was to become a part of.

The authors' love of the theatre is obvious through the tremendous care and attention they have given here to every technical detail — from the scenery and costumes to the stage directions and scenario. An excellent introduction for the beginner and uninitiated to the magic of theatre, while at the same time a fascinating backstage look for those already under its spell, *Make Your Own World of the Theatre* is a fantastic book for all the family. Bravo!

One of my first memories of childhood was the frustration of trying again and again to make my model theatre function in the way that I had seen the live theatre work. Unfortunately I could only concentrate on actually making the wretched thing stand up without falling down. Consequently the productions were not of great quality as my patience was exhausted totally.

Patience, I know, has gone into the making of this book. The detail in every respect is correct and wonderfully executed.

But above all a love of the theatre has been transferred into print by the devotion that has been part of the making of this project.

I can only say that the pleasure which I feel the contents will bring to those who read the book, and make up the models of the Royal Opera House and the two productions, will be a thousand-fold.

Rosemary and Claude have put their hearts into this project, which will be obvious to the reader by its beauty.

HOW TO USE THIS BOOK

This book will make up into a MODEL THEATRE complete with 2 FULL PRODUCTIONS and EIGHT DIFFERENT SETS.
By simply cutting out the pages you will have:
- A three-dimensional THEATRE 27.5 cm × 23 cm (10¾″ × 9″) with backstage details and orchestra ready to cut out, fold and glue.
- TWO PRODUCTIONS:
  - *The Sleeping Beauty.* Ballet in a Prologue and four Acts, five sets, dancers and stage directions.
  - *La Bohème.* Opera in four Acts with three sets, singers and stage directions.
- PROGRAMMES. One for each performance, with authors', composers' and choreographers' biographies and full plots.
- A BOOKLET. Behind the scenes.

GENERAL INSTRUCTIONS FOR MAKING THE THEATRE AND SETS

- You will need:
  - Good sharp, pointed scissors.
  - Tubes of strong, clear glue.
  - Time and patience.
- ALWAYS REMEMBER to:
  - Cut carefully along black lines ——————
  - Fold these lines outwards ·················
  - Fold these lines inwards − − − − − −
  and
  - Glue these areas
  - Pierce holes where shown ○

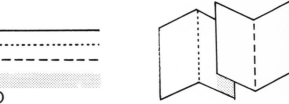

IMPORTANT
- To make folding easier and neater, score along folding lines with the blunt edge of the scissors first.
- Fold the pieces carefully, making sure that you have got folds and shapes correct.
- Matching glue tracks have matching capital letters, numbers or small numbered letters.
- Follow instructions before glueing.
- Follow the page order of the book from beginning to end, starting with the theatre.
- Complete sets are glued to separate stage floors so that once made they can be slid in and out of the theatre.
- Under these stage floors are assembly instructions, so that you can turn the page over for a final check before glueing.
- Stage directions for changing the scenery are behind backcloths together with cast lists, so that you can read them during performances, and there are small numbers on feet flaps of people for you to identify them.

- REMEMBER: When making sets, or giving stage directions, we have specified STAGE LEFT (prompt side) and STAGE RIGHT (opposite prompt) facing out from the stage towards the auditorium.

HOW TO MAKE BOOKLET AND PROGRAMMES
- Cut along the cutting lines on the text pages. Pierce holes where shown. Keep the pages in order. Make the booklet cover by cutting out p. 143 and piercing holes where shown. Bind booklet and programmes either separately or together with paper-fasteners, metal rings or thread ribbon through the holes and tie loosely.

CUT OUT from this side BOOKLET

When we first began work on this project we decided that opera and ballet would be the best subjects because they use large and richly varying dramatic sets and a great deal of costumes and colour.

Sitting not far away from us in London's Covent Garden is the Royal Opera House. Beautiful and accessible. Why not, we asked ourselves, use this magnificent theatre for our model?

We then had to choose which opera and ballet from such an enormous repertoire.

La Bohème with its simple and tragic story of real people is one of the most easily understood and appreciated of operas. The magical *The Sleeping Beauty* with its well-known charming tale of spells and enchantment seemed the ideal ballet.

Obviously we could not use the wonderful elaborate sets and costumes from the Royal Opera House productions by their brilliant and famous designers. We cannot 'fly' the scenery or hang it like the real thing and they would not make up into paper models suitable for this book. So we had to design our own, which we rather enjoyed.

In the case of *La Bohème* we followed Puccini's instructions for the scenery (they are shown in italics in the programme) as he was very definite and precise about what he wanted for his operas. The actions and movements which are described in the programme are again Puccini's own stage directions. We have translated the 'libretto' as closely as possible to the original Italian.

For *The Sleeping Beauty* we had fun designing the sets and costumes with helpful comments from David Wall and his wife Alfreda Thorogood.

As we cannot move tiny paper people on and off stage we have given general tableaux. Thus we show the 'Café Momus' and 'Barrière d'Enfer' scenes with all the participants on stage simultaneously, whereas in reality some would not be there at the same time. This is true also of the ballet where often we have a full stage instead of showing just a few dancers.

We are unable, using paper from this book, to stage the growing foliage in the Palace garden of *The Sleeping Beauty*, nor the cobwebs which fly away when the Princess awakes, nor the upward sweep of the red velvet theatre curtains.

Owing to lack of space we have had to leave out the nymphs from the hunting scene of *The Sleeping Beauty*, the orchestra pit is much smaller than it is in reality and contains less than half the number of musicians. To make the theatre solid we cannot show the horseshoe sweep of the auditorium and have instead folded back the theatre 'boxes' to make strong sides to the model.

By glueing the sets on separate stage floors, you can easily change the scenes by sliding them in and out of the model theatre. We have designed the sets for you to light them with a torch or table lamp from the sides or the front.

Having started this book we soon became engrossed in the life of this great theatre, and the dedicated struggle for perfectionism of the artists who face a highly demanding audience.

In the background, unseen or applauded by the public, are those people who make these complicated performances happen successfully. We have tried, briefly, to speak about them but, alas, this book is too short.

We would like to thank the following people who gave us their help, advice, encouragement and precious time with unstinting generosity:

Ande Anderson, Josephine Barstow, Placido Domingo, Enid Fairhead, Paul Findlay, Arthur Hammond, Trevor Jones, Donald Southern, Nicki Spencer, Alfreda Thorogood and David Wall. Also the other artists and staff whom we pestered for information.

BEHIND THE SCENES

The last members of the audience have been shown to their seats in the auditorium and the Conductor takes his place on the rostrum for the opening bars of music.

After tonight's performance of *La Bohème* the scenery will be put away and the stage and dressing rooms must be empty for tomorrow's rehearsals and the evening performance of *The Sleeping Beauty*. Let us leave the auditorium and go backstage.

After the senior administration staff and directors have decided which opera or ballet they wish to produce, they will have to find out how much it will cost and which singers are available. For opera they will have to be suitable in appearance as well as voice. The best and most attractive singers are in great demand all over the world and have to be booked as long as three years ahead.

The chosen set and costume designer has to study the plot or libretto very carefully so as not to leave out important details, or to put doors in the wrong place. As well as being practical and as cheap as possible, his designs must be imaginative. It may take weeks of searching to find the exact fabrics and dyes for the costumes. These are made and fitted to each artist by expert craftsmen and tailors, and must be easily alterable to fit people of different measurements in case one of the performers has to be replaced through illness or injury. The costumes, no matter how complicated, must also allow the singers and dancers to move freely throughout hot, sweaty, exhausting performances under the batteries of bright lights.

Like the costumes, the wigs are made individually for each artist, using real hair. Beards, moustaches, ringlets, curls and full heads of hair make the performer fit the role to perfection.

La Bohème and *The Sleeping Beauty* will each have over 200 different costumes. Besides cutting out and sewing these detailed and often very beautiful creations, there is the endless cleaning, washing and pressing to make sure that they are fresh for every performance.

For the scenery, the designer's sketches and working drawings are transposed by the Technical Director and his skilled draughtsmen into detailed models, rather like the ones we are making from this book, but complete with lights to confirm the colours of the scenery.

To obtain the most exciting effects a large variety of materials are used for building the sets, but they have to be so light as to be manhandled with ease for scene changes during the intervals.

Shall we take a close look at the stage and scenery?

The stage area must be efficient and uses many modern devices; if you look upwards from the stage to the galleries called the 'flys' you will see a mass of stage machinery. In addition to hanging lights, numerous painted backcloths hang on metal bars from the grid and are 'flown' up and out of sight when not in use. Flats to mask off the side of the stage form part of the scenery and are anchored with weights to the stage when in use. In addition to the flats there are 'trucks', complete scenery units which can be wheeled into position. Whilst moving the scenery during an interval the stage crew has to be as silent as possible. In the wings, rear of the stage, the flys and the dome of the auditorium, closed-circuit television monitors project the Conductor's image to off-stage chorus artists or technicians who cannot see into the orchestra pit.

The Stage Managers who are responsible for the efficient control of the performance as well as checking the entry of artists and many other important details, are based at the control desk in the stage left corner. From here artists are called from their dressing rooms, the curtain is raised and lowered and cues are given to all parts of the stage area and to the lighting control room at the back of the auditorium.

Well, we know now how the designer, technicians and stage crews work, but what about the performers upon whose talents the whole of this complete artistic factory depends? How do they learn their craft?

Some singers start with an intensive course at a college of music and drama. Here young students learn the art of stage presence, movement and speech. There is the extra need to master the foreign languages in which the operas are sung. Training must be long because the voices of singers do not mature early. The handful of great international stars who tour the world making guest appearances are highly paid, but the musical lifespan is pitifully short, lasting only about fifteen years. During that time the strain is constant.

The dancer's body must be trained early, starting sometimes from the age of three. Having passed all the preliminary examinations he or she will then try to join the Royal Ballet junior boarding school at the age of nine or ten for girls, and eleven or twelve for boys. If growth and stamina allow, they then go on to the senior school, with daily classes of four hours' general education and six hours' barre and movement classes. At the age of seventeen or eighteen a talented few are ready for the professional stage.

The singer and dancer are now launched into careers which are hard and demanding. For even the most famous international singer, life is a gruelling round of rehearsals, voice exercises and learning parts, studying scores, endless air-flights, overheated hotel rooms and the constant nursing of the all-important voice.

Singers have to learn as many different opera roles as possible. The world-famous tenor, Placido Domingo, for instance, has eighty-four roles in his repertoire. If necessary, he could fly in and step straight on to the stage of any opera house to replace another singer taken ill. Home and domestic life has somehow to be fitted into this demanding schedule.

The English soprano Josephine Barstow describes her day before a performance in London.

I quite look forward to performance days, they give a wonderful excuse to be shamelessly lazy. I always get up late — usually between 9.30 and 10am and have a lazy breakfast shared with my faithful Westie named Suki. We then potter around the house a bit, poking at pot plants or, if the weather is tempting, maybe doing a little light pruning in the garden. Late morning sees us take a brisk walk, usually shorter than other days, and back to a late lunch. This almost always consists of a starter followed by steak with salad and vegetables and plenty of pasta, rice or potatoes, finishing with fresh fruit and accompanied usually by one or two glasses of red wine. It will be a long time before the curtain goes down, even though I will get a bite to eat during the 'Café Momus' scene in La Bohème.

After lunch I spend up to an hour in bed and then I am ready to go through the score of the evening's opera, usually sitting up in bed. The winding up process to the performance has by now well and truly started and the next task is to give the voice a little gentle exercise, usually for not more than five or ten minutes. A good hot bath follows and then two nice cups of tea and I am then ready to jump into my car and drive to the theatre.

Behind the terror — and that's always there — is the knowledge that you've survived it all before. Now I just want to achieve a little more of the impossible.

For every dancer in the Royal Ballet, each morning begins at the studios with barre work, a series of rigorous exercises to prepare and warm up the muscles and joints for the agonising, arduous leaps and spins. The afternoon is occupied with learning a new ballet, not just one role but two or possibly three, for frequently a dancer may at short notice be expected to replace a colleague with a sprained muscle or ligament. It's an exhausting twelve-hour day by the time the last curtain call is taken at Covent Garden.

A performance of ballet has been described as 'running a three-minute mile with a smile on your face'. Here is how David Wall, internationally famous principal dancer of the Royal Ballet, spends his day before a performance of *The Sleeping Beauty* at Covent Garden.

7.15 The morning of a performance: black coffee, orange juice, cereal then bath. No need to shave — that is done in the afternoon. Dress, then 7.45 walk the two dogs for half an hour, good exercise for all of us. This is when the first thoughts of the evening show first manifest themselves; they very soon disappear as the youngest dog tries to take a bath in the filthy pond opposite the house. 8.15 Another cup of coffee, and get the children loaded into the car ready to drive them to school. Farewells to the beautiful wife (who was principal ballerina and now teaches) and the children's nanny and away we go. Drop children at school and then continue to my place of work, the Royal Ballet Studios. On this leg of the journey, the second thoughts of the pending performance occur; soon quelled as the traffic is so bad that concentration on driving is important if I want to survive.

9.30 One hour of gentle remedial exercising to get the mended and operated parts of the body functioning correctly. 10.30 Company class, which on the day of a show is taken with relaxation and balance in mind; not too much forcing. 11.45–12.15 Class finishes, and half an hour extra of cleaning up and preening the difficult steps and solos of the evening ahead. 12.30 Back home for a light lunch, soup and eggs; perhaps a dessert if the weight is down.

2.00 A little snooze is required (psychological I'm sure). Anxiety about the performance creeps into my head and has to be dealt with by positive thinking. Sleep usually mercifully cuts this process short.

4.00 Awaken for bath and shave. A cup of tea and a biscuit to settle a slightly nervous stomach. 5.00 Leave for the theatre and try to keep the car in the direction of the Royal Opera House, as it tends to want to go home to Tooting quite often. 5.30 Arrive at Stage Door to be greeted by mail and bills. Up to dressing room to start making up and generally repairing facial damage; by 6.30 this is complete, so practice clothes are put on to warm up. This takes place on the stage where the scene is set for the first act.

7.15 Back to the dressing room to put the costume on, and start acting like a prince.

7.30 It all begins. 10.30 The curtain comes down, and after it the gradual winding down of tension.

During the intensive training by singers or dancers in their various studios, the stage in the mornings is alive with the final technical rehearsals of the current production. The stage and lighting experts move in between performances.

While the Lighting Manager gives lighting instructions from the darkened auditorium by loudspeaker to electricians in the upper flys of the stage, the faint sound of music can often be heard from the orchestral rehearsal room.

The hundred-piece orchestra that plays for opera and ballet rehearses under the direction of the Maestro to perfect the work to his interpretation.

The orchestra, lighting technicians and artists perfect their work at independent rehearsals until approximately one week before the first night. The initial attempt on the stage to combine all talent can be fraught with problems. All the diplomacy and energy the Producer can muster, combined with imaginative leadership, must now be used to control as many as 200 artists. With luck the problems may be small: a section of the chorus unable to see the Conductor, a costume too tight, or squeaking sets during a quick change of scenes.

A ballet at this stage usually presents fewer problems than an opera, for not only have the dancers and choreographer adjusted to each other well in advance, but the scenery, taking up less of the stage, presents fewer headaches. The marked studio floor has been transposed to the stage and the dancers in rehearsal count their steps to the full orchestral score instead of to the upright piano.

The dress or final rehearsal usually takes place in the morning, two days before the first night. The pattern is set, the major decisions made, there is no turning back.

This performance is given in its entirety — a run-through without breaks other than intervals. The Producer, Designer, and Stage Director sit at a dimly lit control desk in the auditorium, with a secretary at hand to jot down any final notes.

We have gone through the whole routine of rehearsal and the agonies of production problems. Now it is time for the performance.

LA BOHÈME: Notes

The story of Rodolpho (Rodolphe) in *La Bohème* is to a large extent an autobiographical account of Henri Murger's own life. Born in Paris in February 1822, the son of a concierge who was also a tailor, he was sent to a lawyer's office at the age of fifteen. Devoted equally to liberty and literature he soon left home and joined the Bohemian set of Parisian artists and authors who lived a hand-to-mouth existence in the Latin Quarter. His first book, written in 1843, was unsuccessful and he was saved from destitution by taking a post as secretary, for a while, to Count Tolstoy.

Murger wrote articles for the *Castor* (a journal mentioned in both the book and the opera). A slow, fastidious but temperamental and capricious writer, he first published 'Scenes de la Vie de Bohème' as a series of articles in 1848, the year of Mimi's death. In these 'scenes' he described the loves, amusements and sufferings of a group of impecunious artists and men of letters. The articles were turned into a book and later a play. Murger's excellent descriptions and lively humour, in which he drew a picture of the follies of youth coupled with pathos and tender melancholy, made his work extremely popular. Although he published five other books they did not meet with the same public acclaim.

Money, fame and comfort came too late for Murger. The Bohemian life of hardship and dissipation aggravated by disease caused his early death in a Maison de Santé near Paris in 1861.

Puccini and his librettists amalgamated two of the heroines from Murger's book (Mimi and Francine), and two of Murger's heroes (Rodolphe and Jacques) in order to make his operatic Mimi and Rodolpho more sympathetic and appealing as characters.

Born in Lucca, Italy, in December 1858, Giacomo Puccini was the son of a church organist and born into a musical family. He said of himself that: 'Almighty God touched me with his little finger and said: "Write for the theatre — only for the theatre".' Like Murger, the authenticity of Puccini's music was gained by experience, for many of the incidents described in the opera happened to both. With the composer Mascagni, with whom he shared an apartment, Puccini learnt how to avoid creditors and even sold his overcoat during a freezing winter in Milan in order to take a ballerina out to dinner. In his diary he entered such items as 'Supper for four, one herring'.

He felt passionately about the score of *La Bohème* and demanded nothing short of perfection from his exasperated librettists in his determination to produce an opera that tells a story Puccini himself understood so well.

With its sweeping, glorious melodies, brilliant libretto and colourful score, *La Bohème* portrays characters to whom tragedy occurs in the form of a disease common enough amongst the poor, undernourished people of the time. The composer underlines and illuminates the explosive love of Marcello and Musetta; the gentler, more profound love of Mimi and Rodolpho (though they have their jealousies and quarrels) and the irrepressible humour of Schaunard and Colline.

In each Act these themes of hunger and poverty are set in unifying winter cold. The first two take place on Christmas Eve; in Act 3 we see snow fall; and at the end of Act 4 Mimi's icy hands are warmed by a muff. But at the same time there is, contained in the music, the warmth of love and the gaiety of youth.

La Bohème was first performed in February 1896 at Turin and was not an immediate success. However, three weeks later, when performed with a new cast and conductor, it was then, as now, received with love and acclaim.

Recalling the first performance, many years later, Puccini wrote, 'In the corridors and backstage I heard whispers — "Poor Puccini, this time he's on the wrong track. This opera won't have a long life".'

Puccini's operas were popular and made him a great deal of money, enabling him to indulge in good food, a life of luxury and fast cars. He died in Brussels in November 1924.

THE SLEEPING BEAUTY: Notes

The French author Charles Perrault, 1628–1703 is mostly remembered for his work 'Contes du Temps Passé' written in 1697 which included the stories of the Sleeping Beauty, Red Riding Hood, Bluebeard, Puss-in-Boots and Cinderella. These tales are now so well known and loved that they form part of everyone's childhood.

The Sleeping Beauty owes its existence as the supreme example of Classical ballet to the librettist Vsevolozhsky who was the Director of the Imperial Theatres of Russia for eighteen years from 1881. A charming, cultivated man, he was a friend and mentor to Tchaikovsky and Petipa, encouraging them both to work on the musical score and choreography of *The Sleeping Beauty*. The subject, dear to Vsevolozhsky's heart, was intended as homage to the age of Louis XIV and the glorious court of the French Sun King.

Tchaikovsky certainly needed persuasion. His previous ballet music for *Swan Lake*, composed in 1876 for the Bolshoi Theatre, Moscow, was considered a failure and was never successful until after the composer's death. The conductor and the choreographer neither understood nor appreciated the score, and in order to make the music more acceptable to the public of the time, the conductor butchered the music mercilessly and added works by other composers. Although he had begun to compose a four-act ballet for *Cinderella* before *Swan Lake*, this was never finished and nothing remains now of the music.

Vsevolozhsky was not easily put off, and in his determination to stage *The Sleeping Beauty*, he held endless meetings to bring the composer and choreographer together on the project, designing the costumes himself.

The choreographer Marius Petipa required little encouragement. He knew exactly what he wanted in the way of music for his ballet, giving Tchaikovsky the precise number of measures he needed, what tempo, style and even the orchestral score for each of the variations and episodes. During a rehearsal the music ran out before the painted panorama of the Lakeside scene in Act 2 had finished rolling its full length. Tchaikovsky had to compose as many new bars of music as there were extra metres of canvas.

Of these three determined and dedicated men, the contributions were thus united; Vsevolozhsky, with his conception of royal pageant at the end of the ballet (with Apollo dressed as the Sun King in the original version); Petipa with his brilliant and decisive dance sequences; and Tchaikovsky who put all his heart into the ballet music.

Tchaikovsky loved this romantic tale and illustrated the story of the Sleeping Princess and the triumph of good over evil with strong emotional music, full of vitality and evocative melodies.

The music for *The Sleeping Beauty* was Tchaikovsky's own favourite ballet score, and it is easy to understand why, although at the first general rehearsal, which took place at the Maryinski Theatre St Petersburg in front of the Tsar and court, the work was received very coolly. Tchaikovsky recorded in his diary, 'Rehearsal of the ballet with the Tzar present, "Very nice!!!" His Majesty treated me very haughtily. God bless him'.

HOW TO MAKE THE THEATRE

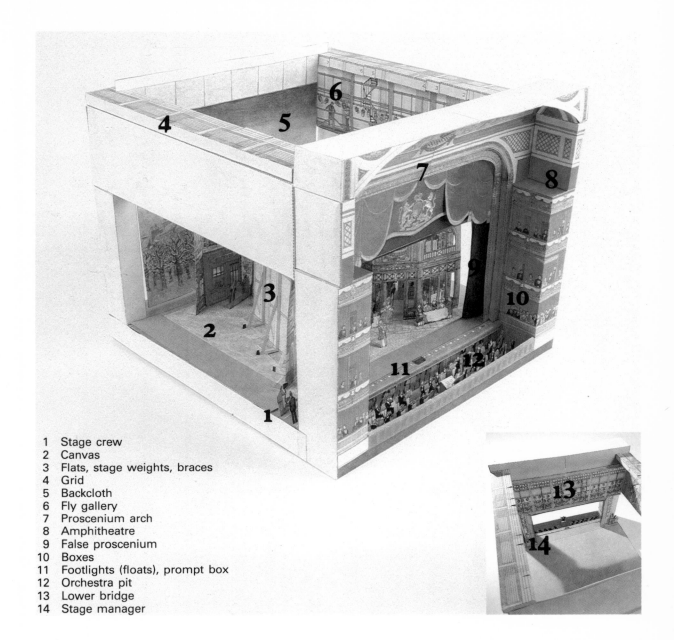

1 Stage crew
2 Canvas
3 Flats, stage weights, braces
4 Grid
5 Backcloth
6 Fly gallery
7 Proscenium arch
8 Amphitheatre
9 False proscenium
10 Boxes
11 Footlights (floats), prompt box
12 Orchestra pit
13 Lower bridge
14 Stage manager

LOOK CAREFULLY AT THE PICTURE OF THE FINISHED THEATRE

CUTTING AND FOLDING
- Cut out and fold pieces as shown on page 5.
- Before glueing make sure that the folded pieces match the shapes of the finished model.

ASSEMBLY
- There are numbered letters to help you match up glue tracks; these tell you the order for glueing. For example, A1 to A1, then A2 to A2 etc ... They also indicate the various levels and parts of the theatre: A = Base, floor, orchestra pit. B = Tiers of boxes. C = Amphitheatre level. D = Theatre ceiling. E = False proscenium. F = Fly galleries and lower bridge (lighting). G = Grid.

BUILD THE THEATRE, STEP BY STEP, in the following order:

FLOOR BASE
- Fold and glue: front section p. 13, back section p. 15, stage left p. 17, stage right p. 19.
- Glue side sections to front and back sections A1, A2, A3, A4 to make base.
- Glue stage floor onto base A5, A6, A7, A8.
- Glue A9 (orchestra pit floor) to A9 underneath base.

PROSCENIUM
- Fold proscenium arch and glue to proscenium wall, stage left (both on p. 25).
- Fold proscenium arch and glue to proscenium wall, stage right (both on p. 27).
- Glue both halves of proscenium together.
- Glue back of proscenium to front of stage A10, A11.

BOXES
- Fold boxes, glue to proscenium wall B1, B2 and orchestra pit floor A12 stage left.
- Fold boxes and glue to proscenium wall B3, B4 and orchestra pit floor A13 stage right.

ORCHESTRA PIT
- Fold back and glue front of orchestra pit to boxes A14, A15.

THEATRE BASE TRIM
- Glue trim to sides of base, stage left A15, A17, stage right A18, A19.

PELMET FOR HOUSE CURTAINS (TABS)
- Glue both halves of the pelmet to back of proscenium arch.
- Glue coat of arms to back of pelmet.

FOOTLIGHTS (FLOATS)
- Fold back and glue footlights A22 to orchestra pit back wall, then to stage floor.

AMPHITHEATRE
- Fold and glue amphitheatre wall stage left C2.
- Fold and glue amphitheatre wall stage right C4.
- Glue in the following order the two finished amphitheatre sections:
  - Stage right C3 to top of boxes C3, C4 to proscenium wall C4.
  - Stage left C1 to top of boxes C1, C2 to proscenium wall C2.

PROSCENIUM ROOF
- Fold and glue the proscenium roof D2 and D4 to back of frieze.
- Fold and glue frieze glue tracks to proscenium roof.

CEILING
- Fold and glue theatre ceiling to top of amphitheatre wall stage left D1 to D1.
- Glue theatre ceiling to top of proscenium roof along glue track.
- Fold and glue theatre ceiling to top of amphitheatre wall stage right D3 to D3.
- Glue theatre ceiling to top of proscenium roof along glue track.
- Fold back the two sections' tops, glue together and glue to back of proscenium.

NOW THAT THE AUDITORIUM SIDE OF THE THEATRE IS FINISHED WE GO BACKSTAGE

FALSE PROSCENIUM
- Fold and glue to stage floor, where indicated, and to back of proscenium wall E1 to E2 and E2 to E1.

REAR COLUMNS
- Fold and glue columns, glue to stage floor stage left A20, stage right A21.

FLY GALLERIES
- Fold and glue fly galleries
- Glue to back of proscenium and to top of columns stage left F1, F2 and stage right F3, F4.

LOWER BRIDGE (LIGHTING)
- Fold and glue bridge. Glue to back of false proscenium F5 and to fly galleries F6, F7.

GRID
- Cut along black lines numbered slits 1 to 8, on both sections G1, G2.
- Fold and glue grid stage left G1, stage right G2.
- Glue grid to top of fly gallery and back of proscenium wall stage left G1, G3.
- Glue grid to top of fly gallery and back of proscenium wall stage right G2, G4.

BACK OF THEATRE
- Glue theatre back wall to fly galleries F8 and F9.

STAGE CREW
- Fold flaps back, glue along lines on stage floor behind proscenium, on top of the small matching numbers.

ORCHESTRA
- Fold flaps back, glue along lines on orchestra pit floor, on top of matching numbers.

CONDUCTOR
- Fold and glue Conductor's rostrum, glue to orchestra pit floor where indicated.

THEATRE CURTAINS (TABS)
- Glue Tabs (p. 11) to hanger (p. 23) along glue track.
- Drop Tabs into grid slot 1.

NOW YOU HAVE BUILT THE THEATRE, IT IS TIME TO MAKE UP THE SETS AND CASTS

CUT OUT from this side   Theatre rear columns; footlights ('floats')

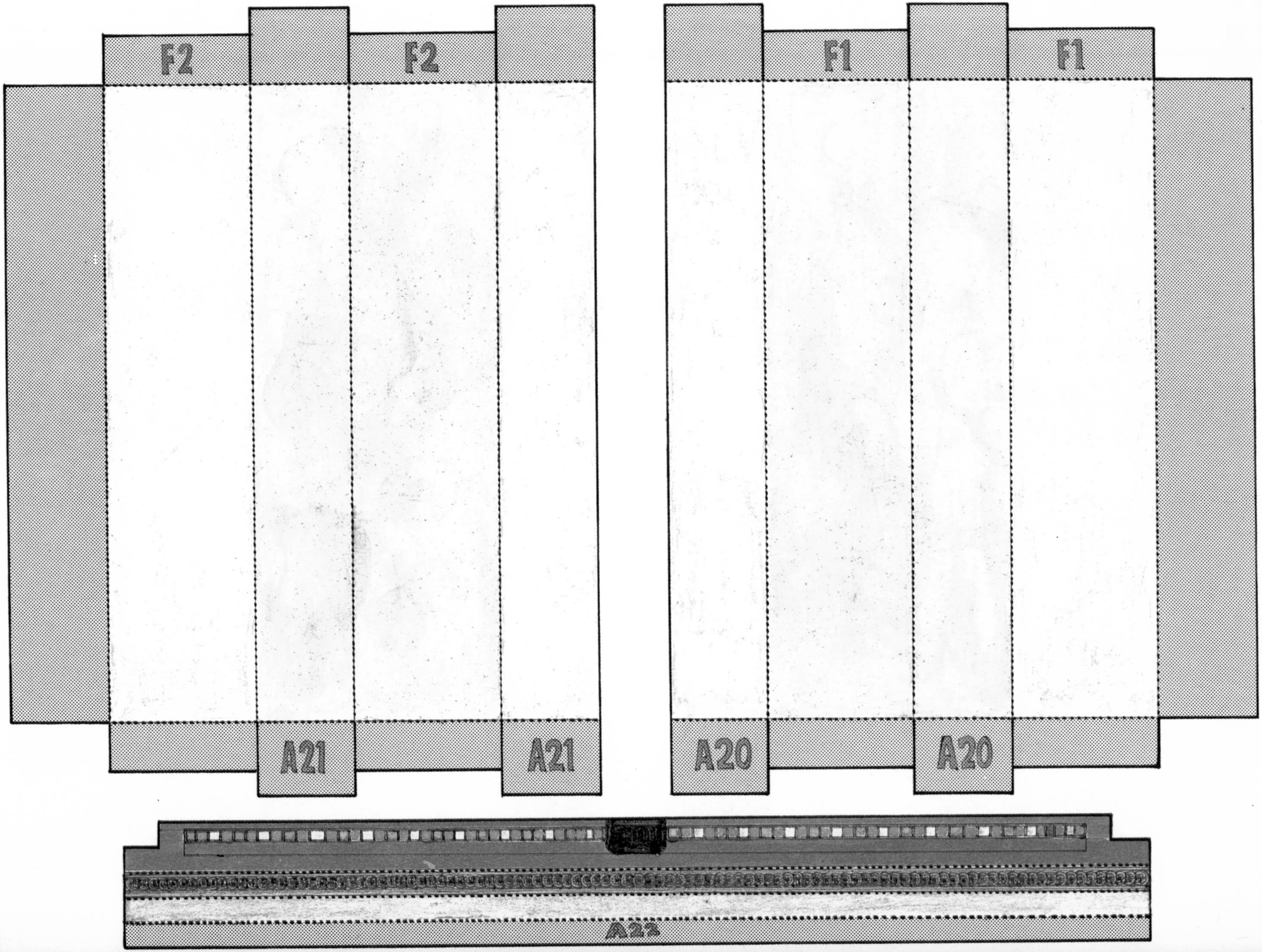

F1

F1

A20

A20

A21

F2

A21

F2

A22

37

38

DO NOT CUT OUT from this side

F2

F2

F6

F1

G1

F8

F8

39

40

DO NOT CUT OUT from this side

F9

F3

F9

F3

G2

F7

F4 F9

F4

42

F7

F7

F6

F8

F9

F5

CUT OUT from this side – The grid: stage left section G1, stage right section G2

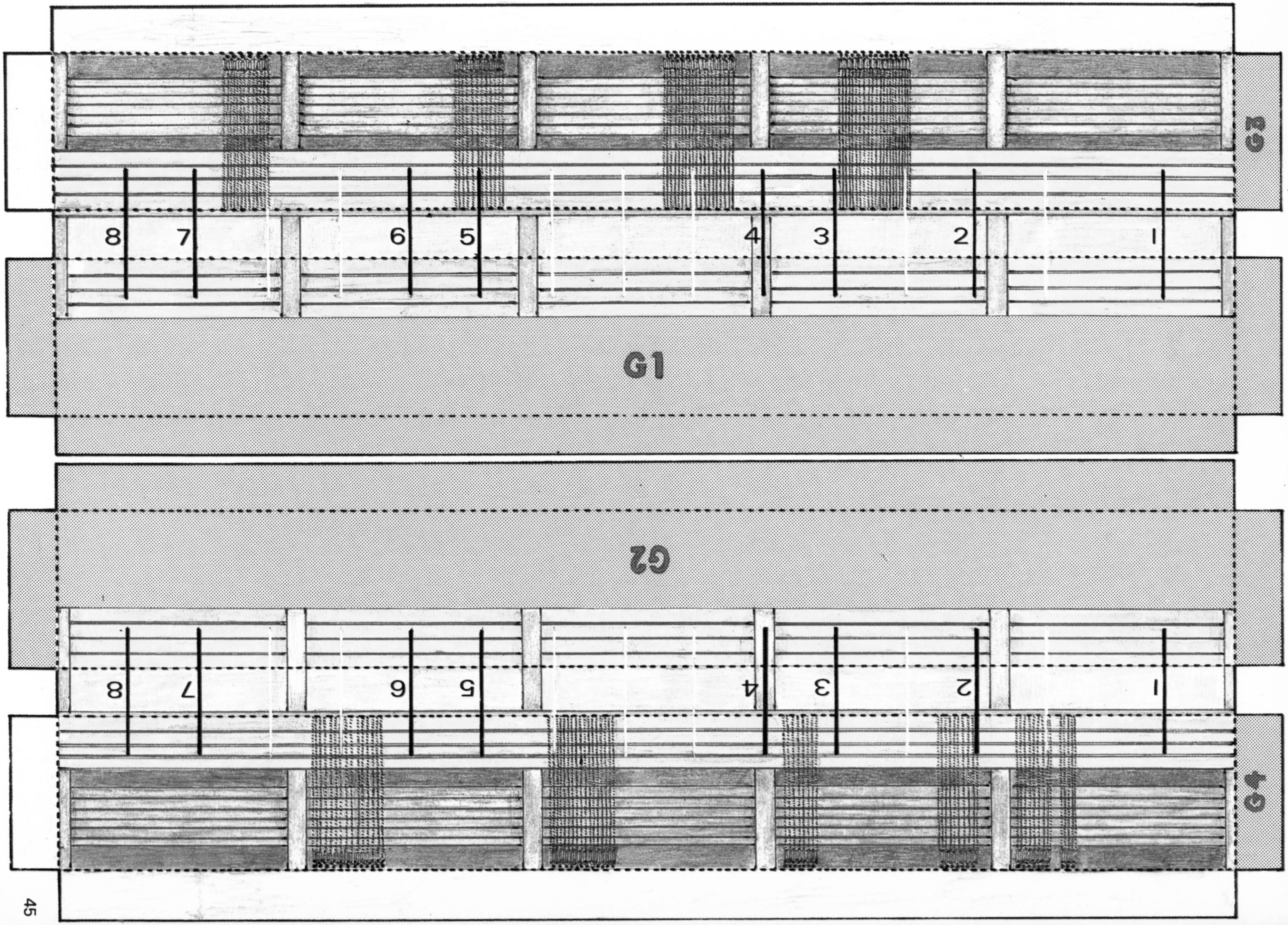

LA BOHEME
Opera in four acts

Music by Giacomo PUCCINI
Libretto by Giuseppe Giacosa and Luigi Illica

From "Scènes de la vie de Bohème" by Henri MURGER

Rodolpho, a poet . . . . Tenor
Marcello, a painter . . . . Baritone
Colline, a philosopher . . . . Bass
Schaunard, a musician . . . . . Baritone
Benoit, their landlord . . . . Bass

Mimi . . . . Soprano
Musetta, a grisette . . . . Soprano
Alcindoro, a Councillor of State   Bass
Parpignol, a street toy-seller . . . Tenor

Place: The Latin Quarter of Paris. Time: about 1840

ACT 1: In a Paris attic around 1840

A broad window from which can be seen an expanse of snow-covered roofs. Left, a stove. A table, a cupboard, a small bookcase, four chairs, an easel with a sketched-out canvas and a stool, a bed, some scattered books, several bundles of paper, two candlesticks. A door at the centre, another on the left.

As the opera begins Rodolpho is gazing thoughtfully out of the window. Marcello is working on his picture 'The Crossing of the Red Sea', his hands numb with the intense cold. It is Christmas Eve. Marcello complains that he is as damp and chilly as if the Red Sea was dripping down his back. Rodolpho enviously watches the smoke rising into the grey sky from the thousand little chimneys of Paris and eyes their own empty stove with contempt.

Laying aside palette and brushes, Marcello grumbles that his fingers are as icy as Musetta's heart. Seizing a chair he is about to break it into pieces for firewood, when Rodolpho takes a bulky notebook from the table and suggests they burn his play instead. Marcello nobly offers to burn the 'Red Sea' but Rodolpho protests that the canvas would stink. 'No,' insists Rodolpho, 'my ardent drama will warm us!' Giving Marcello part of the manuscript he says, 'You take Act 1'. They tear up the manuscript, thrust it into the stove, set fire to it and sit down to warm themselves by the flames.

Colline, the philosopher, bursts in noisily and angrily throws down a bundle of books tied in a handkerchief announcing that all the pawnshops are closed because it is Christmas Eve. He breaks off in delight when he sees the fire, and grabbing Rodolpho's chair, joins the poet and painter around the stove. Rodolpho tears up the remaining Acts while Marcello and Colline agree that although the play is going out in a blaze of glory, it is too short and has no real staying power. 'Down with the author!' they shout as the embers die.

At that moment, to their amazement, two shop boys come through the door; one carrying food, cigars and bottles of wine, the other a bundle of firewood. The welcome arrival of these provisions is explained by the triumphant entrance of the musician Schaunard who throws some coins on the floor. This sudden wealth, he explains, is his fee for a ridiculous commission and proceeds to tell his story.

Schaunard's tale goes unheeded by the other Bohemians who are far too busy kindling a large fire in the stove. They have already started to eat the pastries when Schaunard, seeing that no one is paying any attention to him, seizes Colline as he passes with a plate.

'What are you up to?' he cries. 'These provisions are stores for the dark and gloomy future!' He clears the food from the table and puts it in the cupboard declaring that they should all celebrate Christmas Eve in the Latin Quarter. 'We may drink indoors, but we are dining out!' The others agree enthusiastically, Rodolpho locks the door, and they all gather round the table and pour out the wine.

Suddenly, there are two sharp knocks at the door. It is the old landlord, Benoit, who has come for the quarterly rent. After consulting the others Schaunard opens the door and to Benoit's surprise the four Bohemians not only courteously offer him a seat but also ply him with wine. He shows Marcello the rent demand and Marcello grandly shows him the money on the table. 'Have you gone mad?' hisses Schaunard but Marcello continues to placate Benoit. 'You see it?' he asks. 'Well then, stop worrying and join our party for a while.' They refill the landlord's glass and Marcello goes on to mention the pretty young redhead he saw in Benoit's company the other night. The wine and flattery soon turn the landlord's head and he begins to boast about his flirtations, confessing his weakness for lively, plump young girls; thin women like his wife are troublesome, always whining and nagging...

This is just what Marcello has been waiting for; feigning great moral indignation, he bangs his fist on the table and jumps to his feet. The others follow his example. 'For shame,' they cry, 'he's corrupting our respectable home.' Benoit protests, but the outraged Bohemians encircle him and push him out of the door.

'That's paid the quarter's rent!' announces Marcello with satisfaction.

The four, delighted with the success of their ruse, decide to spend the evening at the Café Momus and, dividing Schaunard's money between them, prepare to leave at once. Rodolpho stays behind to finish an article he is writing for a journal. It will only take a few minutes, he assures them, and the others promise to wait for him downstairs at the porter's lodge. Rodolpho stands on the landing holding a candle to light them down the dark, rickety staircase, but Colline takes a tumble. 'Are you dead, Colline?' Rodolpho calls down. 'Not yet,' retorts Colline. Clearing a corner of the table and taking inkstand and paper, Rodolpho starts to write. He stops and starts again, tears up the paper, then

impatiently throws aside the pen declaring that he is not in the mood.

Just then, there is a timid knock at the door. 'Who's there?' calls Rodolpho. 'Excuse me, forgive me, but my candle has gone out,' a girl's voice replies. Rodolpho runs to open the door and at the threshold, holding her unlit candle and key, stands Mimi. Rodolpho invites her to come in, but as she does so she is overcome by a bout of coughing and he is appalled to see how ill she looks. 'I'm out of breath . . . that staircase!' she gasps. Rodolpho fetches some water which he sprinkles on her pale face to revive her. She comes to, and he asks anxiously if she feels better. 'Come nearer the fire,' he urges. 'A drop of wine?' She accepts gratefully and as she sips he notices how remarkably pretty she is. When the young woman has fully recovered, Rodolpho lights her candle and accompanies her to the door, before returning to his work.

A few minutes later, however, Mimi reappears in the doorway. 'How absent-minded I am! My door key. Where did I leave it?'

'Don't stand in the draught, your candle's flickering,' warns Rodolpho, but too late for it has blown out. He hurries to light hers with his own, but as he nears the door his candle is blown out too, and the room is plunged into darkness.

'I'm a tiresome neighbour,' Mimi apologises as together she and Rodolpho go down on their hands and knees to search for the key. 'Ah!' exclaims Rodolpho as he finds the key and quickly conceals it in his pocket. 'Have you found it?' inquires Mimi. 'No,' lies Rodolpho, pretending to search but all the while approaching Mimi guided by her voice. Their hands meet and he takes hold of hers and does not let go.

'How cold this little hand is!' he says. 'Let me warm it for you. It is hopeless searching here in the dark, we'll find nothing; but with good luck there will be a bright moon tonight and up here the moon is our next-door neighbour.'

'May I tell you who I am and what I do?' he asks.

As Mimi nods her assent, he tells her that he is a poet and manages to scrape a living somehow by writing; though financially poor, he is rich in dreams and castles in the air.

'Now that you know about me, tell me who you are,' he urges.

Shyly the young woman tells him that she is always called Mimi although her real name is Lucille. Her story, she says, is a short one. She embroiders on linen or silk, her life is quiet and happy for she enjoys sewing roses and lilies as they remind her of love and spring-time, of dreams and romances. She prepares simple meals for herself and does not always go to Mass, although she often prays. Her little, white attic room looks out over the roofs and sky but when the thaw comes the first sunshine is hers and the first kiss of April too! She loves the scent of real roses, but alas, the ones she makes have none.

'There is no more I can say about myself,' she ends simply, 'I am just your neighbour who has come in and disturbed you.'

From the courtyard below his impatient friends shout to Rodolpho to hurry. He crosses to the window and opens it. 'I've still three lines to write,' he calls down. 'There are two of us — go ahead to Momus and keep us places, we'll be there soon.'

The moonlight streams into the room and Rodolpho remains at the window to make sure that his friends have gone. Mimi comes nearer, and turning round, Rodolpho sees her sweet face bathed in soft light; he falls in love with her and she with him.

Arm-in-arm they leave the attic and go out into the night to join the other Bohemians at the Café Momus.

ACT 2: In the Latin Quarter

A crossroad which opens out on to a square; shops of all kinds; on one side the Café Momus. A large motley crowd of townsfolk, soldiers, servant girls, children, students, seam-stresses, gendarmes, etc. The stalls are lit with lamps and lanterns; a large lantern illuminates the entrance to the Café.

As the curtain goes up the stage is full of noise and bustle. Urchins, hawkers and vendors shout out their wares.

The customers at the Café Momus call their orders to the waiter and being Christmas Eve it is so full that some customers have had to be seated outside. Amongst the crowd the Bohemians and Mimi are celebrating their small fortune by spending it on presents for themselves. Schaunard buys a cheap French hunting horn and a pipe from a scrap metal shop. Colline too gets a bargain — a secondhand coat from the clothes-repairer's shop, well worn but it contains capacious pockets into which he immediately stuffs his books. Rodolpho takes Mimi into a milliner's shop to buy her a bonnet. Marcello, a parcel under his arm, flirts with the girls who are pushed against him by the jostling hordes.

Schaunard is first to arrive at the Café Momus where he waits for his friends, soon to be joined by Colline, delightedly waving his latest find — a rare old book of runic grammar. Marcello turns up hungry and impatient to eat. As the noisy Bohemians collect a table from inside the Café and set it on the pavement, Rodolpho and Mimi leave the milliner's shop. Mimi, contentedly clutching a small parcel, pauses to watch a group of students.

'Who are you looking at?' demands Rodolpho.

'Are you jealous?' she teases.

'A man in love is easily jealous,' he mutters.

On reaching the Café Momus Rodolpho introduces Mimi to his friends.

'Songs blossom from my brain, flowers blossom from her fingers, from exultant souls blossoms love!' he announces grandly.

'Heavens,' snorts Marcello, 'what flowery language!'

Whilst they order a lavish supper, the toy seller Parpignol comes into the square. His barrow, lit by Chinese lanterns, is surrounded by excited children. They dance round him pointing at the toys. 'I want the trumpet and the horse!' 'The tambourine!' 'I want the gun!' 'I want the whip and the platoon of soldiers!' Angry mothers appear looking for their children, and try to drag them away but have to relent. Parpignol moves on down the street followed by the noisy, merry youngsters.

When Marcello can make himself heard he asks Mimi what Rodolpho has bought her. Taking a lace-trimmed bonnet from the parcel, she shows it to him proudly.

'Oh lovely age of deception and idealism, when you trust and hope and everything seems beautiful,' murmurs Marcello, gazing at her happy face. His remark sparks off a joyful philosophical train of thought amongst the friends.

'Away with sorrow, let's drink!' they shout, jumping to their feet.

'Give me a phial of poison,' chokes Marcello as his flamboyant former mistress Musetta appears at the corner of the street. Behind Musetta, trying to keep up with her, puffs the pompous old Councillor Alcindoro. 'Come along Lulu,' she laughs, as though he were a pet dog.

Musetta notices the Bohemians (especially Marcello) at the Café and motions Alcindoro to sit down at the table next to theirs, so that she and Marcello have a clear view of each other. 'What, outside here?' grumbles Alcindoro. 'Sit down Lulu,' commands Musetta as the Councillor sits down, crossly turning up his coat collar against the cold. Seeing that the friends are pretending to take no notice of her, Musetta decides to make a fuss to attract Marcello's attention. She sniffs at her plate and shrieking 'Hey, waiter! This plate reeks of grease!' throws it on the ground. The waiter picks up the pieces while Alcindoro, embarrassed, begs her to be quiet. But Musetta gets more and more angry at Marcello's indifference. Alcindoro, worried for his position and reputation, nervously takes the menu and tries to order supper. 'Do talk quietly,' he beseeches her. 'I'll behave how I like, don't be a bore,' she snaps. Then shouts at the top of her voice to Marcello, 'Why won't you look at me?'

'But you can see that I'm giving the order,' mumbles Alcindoro placatingly, thinking that she is talking to him.

Schaunard and Colline find the whole situation hilarious and keep up a running commentary. 'She speaks to one, so that the other can listen,' chuckles Schaunard as poor Marcello becomes more agitated. Musetta seeing this launches into her favourite waltz song, 'When I walk along down the street, people turn to admire my beauty.' She stands up and waltzes round singing whilst Alcindoro begs her to resume her seat. But Musetta is in full cry and nothing can stop her. 'I know,' she continues, looking at Marcello, 'that you would rather die than confess your torment.' As Marcello struggles to remain indifferent and Mimi murmurs to Rodolpho that it is obvious Musetta loves the painter, Rodolpho explains that she left Marcello in order to lead a more luxurious life.

As Alcindoro pleads with her to be more discreet Musetta decides she must get rid of the old fool. Pretending to have a pain in her foot she suddenly lets out a piercing scream and hops to a chair. 'What pain! What agony!' She takes off her shoe and giving it to Alcindoro sends him away to a cobbler to buy a new pair. The Councillor hides the shoe under his jacket and hurries off. No sooner has he disappeared than Musetta and Marcello rush laughing into each other's arms.

The Bohemians' laughter soon ceases, however, when the waiter presents them with the bill, which they pass round, searching their pockets for money. Rodolpho has only thirty sous left and the others have nothing. Musetta has a brainwave and asks for Alcindoro's bill. In the distance marching soldiers and a military band are heard approaching, windows open and mothers and children appear on doorsteps and balconies eagerly awaiting the patrol.

Musetta puts the two bills together placing them on Alcindoro's table and the Bohemians reassure the waiter that the old gentleman will pay.

They look for a means of escape. 'This dense crowd will give us cover!' exclaim the Bohemians as the patrol enters, headed by a handsome drum major twirling his baton. To the delight of the crowd Musetta, who cannot walk with only one shoe, is lifted on to the shoulders of Marcello and Colline, who break through the spectators and follow the patrol. Rodolpho and Mimi follow arm-in-arm and finally Schaunard with his horn to his lips, as everyone falls in behind the patrol and marches off into the distance.

Alcindoro, with a pair of new shoes, returns to the Café Momus and looks for Musetta. The waiter presents both bills to Alcindoro who, seeing the amount and finding himself deserted, sinks into a chair, flabbergasted.

ACT 3: The Barrière d'enfer

Beyond the toll gate lies the outer boulevard, and in the distance the Route d'Orleans is lost in the mist and fog of February. This side of the toll gate, on the left, is a tavern and a small open space. Snow is falling. The tavern has as its sign Marcello's picture 'The Crossing of the Red Sea'. On either side of the door are frescoes of a Turk and a zouave with an enormous laurel wreath around his fez. Light streams from windows on the ground floor. Tall, grey plane trees stretch diagonally towards the boulevard, between the trees are marble benches. As the curtain rises the scene is bathed in the uncertain light of first dawn. In front of a brazier customs officials are sitting dozing. From the tavern come shouts, laughter and the clink of glasses. The toll barrier is closed.

Street sweepers behind the gate stamp their feet in the snow. 'Hey there guards, open up!' There's no response so they bang their brooms against the railings and shout again. One of the customs officials stretches, gets up and opens the gate for the sweepers to pass through.

From the tavern Musetta can be heard singing with the customers.

Carters and milkwomen are coming into Paris from the country. They are checked at the gate and allowed in, followed by peasant women carrying baskets on their arms and calling out their wares as they move off into the city in different directions.

Mimi enters, unsure of her whereabouts, and asks a servant girl from the tavern to find Marcello as she must speak to him urgently. Marcello, surprised to see Mimi, explains that he and Musetta have been living free at the inn for the past month. Musetta teaches singing to the patrons whilst he paints soldiers on the house-front. 'It's cold, come inside,' he urges as Mimi begins to cough, but when he tells her that Rodolpho is there also, she refuses. 'Why not?' he asks.

'Oh Marcello, help me,' cries Mimi and bursts into tears. She tells him how Rodolpho loves her but is consumed by jealousy. He keeps telling her to find another lover.

'When it's like that two people cannot live together,' admits Marcello.

'You're right, I should leave him,' agrees Mimi sorrowfully.

Marcello says that Rodolpho came to the tavern before daylight, dropped on a bench and fell asleep. Coughing badly, Mimi looks through the window to see him. She manages to tell Marcello that Rodolpho left her the previous night, saying that it was all over between them. As Rodolpho begins to wake up, Marcello urges Mimi to hide and not to make a scene. Pushing her gently away he goes to meet Rodolpho as he emerges from the tavern.

Rodolpho tells Marcello that he and Mimi have quarrelled and must separate. She flirts with everyone, he says, and a foppish young Viscount is making eyes at her. Marcello, unconvinced, accuses Rodolpho of being jealous, tiresome and stubborn. Rodolpho confesses that this is not the entire truth. In fact, he loves Mimi more than anything on earth but he is afraid . . . Hearing this, Mimi slips nearer, hiding behind a tree.

'Mimi is so ill, she grows weaker every day,' Rodolpho confesses, 'the poor child is dying.' He describes her dreadful cough, thin body and burning fever, all aggravated by his cold, miserable lodgings. He blames his poverty for her condition. 'It's my fault,' he says, 'love alone is not enough to bring her back to life.'

All this is overheard by the frightened Mimi whose pathetic sobbing gives her away. Rodolpho rushes to her and, taking her in his arms, assures her that he has been exaggerating.

Musetta's laughter comes ringing from the tavern and Marcello runs in to find out what she is up to.

Mimi tells Rodolpho that she is leaving him. They must part without bitterness. She will send someone to collect her few possessions but the bonnet under her pillow — perhaps he would like to keep it as a reminder of their love?

With sadness they say farewell to the happiness, kisses and quarrels of their life together.

From inside the tavern a sudden commotion of crashing plates, breaking glasses and angrily raised voices signal a furious argument between Marcello and Musetta. Musetta comes flouncing out followed by Marcello.

'I'll give you a thrashing if I find you flirting again,' he yells.

'What are you making all this song and dance about? We haven't been tied up at the altar!' retorts Musetta. 'I can flirt with whom I please!' The couple continue to hurl insults at each other until Musetta runs off, turning to scream 'Shop painter!'

'Viper!'

'Toad!'

'Witch!' snarls Marcello storming back into the tavern.

Whilst the painter and his mistress have been quarrelling Rodolpho and Mimi have decided that it is too hard to separate in winter, to be alone and cold. Springtime makes unhappiness easier to bear; they will part when the flowers bloom again.

ACT 4: In the attic several months later

Marcello again stands at his easel, and Rodolpho sits at his table, each putting on a show of working indefatigably.

Rodolpho announces that he has seen Musetta riding in a carriage and pair complete with footmen. Marcello, forcing a laugh, pretends not to care, and mentions that he has seen Mimi also riding in a carriage, dressed like a queen. To which Rodolpho retorts that he's glad to hear it and they both continue to work feverishly — but not for long.

Unseen by Rodolpho, Marcello takes a silk ribbon from his pocket and kisses it, then putting it away stares at his canvas. Rodolpho, deep in thought, secretly takes Mimi's bonnet from the table drawer. Marcello finds that he can paint nothing but Musetta's face, and Rodolpho can think only of his happiness with Mimi.

Trying to conceal his emotion from Marcello, Rodolpho asks Marcello what time it is. 'Time for yesterday's dinner,' replies Marcello. 'But Schaunard is not back yet,' Rodolpho points out. No sooner has he spoken than Schaunard enters with four small loaves, followed by Colline carrying a paper bag. 'Gentlemen, dinner is served!' announces Colline proudly, placing one salt herring on the table. 'A feast for the Gods!' remarks Marcello, 'we must put the champagne on ice,' and he puts a bottle of water in Colline's battered top-hat. A single tumbler is passed round with great ceremony until Schaunard climbs on a chair and solemnly starts to make a speech. The others interrupt him and suggest some dancing instead — some ballet, a minuet, a fandango. Then, as they take their partners for the quadrille, Rodolpho bows low to Marcello murmuring gallantly, 'Enchanting maiden!' Marcello, in a bashful falsetto, squeaks, 'Respect my modesty, sir!' The dance soon degenerates into horseplay when Schaunard tells Colline that he has the manners of a clod. Colline seizes the fire-tongs and shouts, 'Draw your sword!' Grasping the shovel, Schaunard adopts a fencing posture, retorting, 'I will drink your blood!' Armed with the fire-irons, the pair caper around the room.

At the height of the uproar, the door bursts open and Musetta rushes in, in a state of great agitation.

'It's Mimi, she's very ill . . . she climbed the staircase but can go no further.'

Through the open doorway Mimi can be seen sitting on the top stair. Marcello and Rodolpho half lead, half carry Mimi to the bed. Taking the tumbler Musetta gives Mimi some water.

'Oh my Rodolpho, may I stay here with you?' asks Mimi.

'Always!' replies Rodolpho. He persuades her to lie down, draws the coverlet over her and carefully puts the pillow under her head.

Musetta, taking the others aside, explains that she had heard that Mimi had left the Viscount with whom she was living, and was dying of consumption. Not knowing where Mimi had gone, Musetta had searched everywhere and had only just found her. Mimi had told her, 'I'm finished. I'm dying. I know it. I want to die near him. Perhaps he's waiting for me.'

The Bohemians have nothing to give poor Mimi. There is no coffee, no wine, in the attic. Musetta draws Marcello away from Mimi and, removing her earrings, gives them to him, telling him to sell them to buy medicine and to send for a doctor.

'I feel so cold,' whispers Mimi, 'if only I had a muff.'

Rodolpho takes her hands in his to warm them.

'Don't talk,' he urges. Mimi, reassuring him that she speaks quietly, tells Marcello how kind Musetta is. Musetta stops Marcello just as he is about to leave. 'One moment,' she says, 'perhaps this is her last wish; I'll go with you and get her a muff,' and they hurry out.

Meanwhile, Colline takes off his beloved old overcoat and bids it a solemn farewell. He folds up the coat, puts it under his arm and is about to go out, but seeing Schaunard touches him on the shoulder, saying, 'Let us both do a good deed. I'm going to pawn this coat, you must leave these two alone.'

'Of course,' agrees Schaunard and taking the empty water bottle as an excuse he follows Colline, closing the door carefully.

'Have they gone?' asks Mimi. 'I pretended to be asleep because I wanted to be alone with you. There are so many things I want to say to you.' Rodolpho takes the bonnet from his pocket and places it gently on her head. 'Do you remember the first time I came here?' she asks. 'My candle had gone out.' 'Then you lost your key,' Rodolpho reminds her. 'I can tell you now, sir, I know you found it very quickly,' smiles Mimi. 'It was dark, and you took my hand.' Mimi is suddenly seized by a violent coughing spasm which takes her breath away. Rodolpho holds her close, crying, 'Oh God! Mimi!' Hearing Rodolpho cry out Schaunard rushes in and hurries over to the bed, but Mimi tells him that it is nothing. Musetta and Marcello return and enter cautiously; she carries a muff and a medicine bottle. 'Is she asleep?' asks Musetta. 'She's resting,' Rodolpho answers. Marcello says he has seen the doctor who will be coming soon, and taking a spirit lamp, he lights it to heat up the medicine.

Musetta gives Mimi the muff. 'How lovely and soft it is!' she murmurs. 'My hands will not be icy any more. Was it you who gave it to me?' she asks Rodolpho. 'Yes,' replies Musetta promptly. 'You spendthrift!' Mimi chides him. 'Thank you, but it was expensive! Don't cry, I'm better now. Why do you weep so? My hands are warmer and I shall sleep a little.'

Putting her hands in the muff, Mimi gradually falls asleep, her head droops forward and her cheek rests on the fur muff.

Musetta heats the medicine on the spirit lamp, quietly uttering a prayer, as Marcello shields the flame to stop it from flickering. While Rodolpho goes over to Musetta to look at the medicine, Schaunard, on tiptoe, crosses the room to Mimi. He turns to Marcello with a shocked expression and says quietly, 'Marcello, she is gone!'

A bright ray of sunlight shines through the window on to Mimi's face. Musetta points to her cloak and Rodolpho takes it and stands on a chair contemplating how best to shade the window. Colline returns with the money, giving it to Musetta to buy food, and goes to help Rodolpho hang the cloak. 'How is she?' he asks. 'As you can see, she's sleeping,' Rodolpho replies. Musetta makes a sign that the medicine is ready and getting down from his chair Rodolpho goes towards her. As he does so, he catches sight of Marcello and Schaunard's shocked faces.

'Why do you look at me like that?' he cries, glancing from one to the other. Marcello puts a comforting arm round his shoulder.

'Courage!' he urges as Rodolpho, realising that she is dead, rushes to kneel, sobbing, beside the bed of his beloved Mimi.

Murger's book was based on facts and real characters. Schaunard was Alexandre Schanne, a painter and composer who played the French hunting horn. A publisher's misprint changed his name from Murger's *Schannard* to Schaunard. Marcello (Marcel) was based on the painter Tabar who started a canvas called 'The Passage of the Red Sea' which he had to give up because he could not pay for models. It was said that Tabar's painting was submitted to, and rejected by, the Salon so many times that it could find its own way there and back. Musetta (Musette — bagpipe) was so called because of the pitch and stridency of her voice. She earned a living in the same irregular way as her operatic counterpart, eventually becoming quite rich. She left Paris, taking all her money, and sailed from Marseilles to join her married sister in Algeria. The packet boat *Atlas* sank in 1863 in the Mediterranean drowning Musetta, her worldly goods and 200 other passengers.

The character of Colline was based on two authors of theological books — one possessing a famous great coat, the four pockets of which were so crammed full of books that each of the pockets was named after the public libraries of Paris. Mimi, whose real name was Lucille Louvet, was an artificial flower-maker, and a girlfriend of Murger. She died of tuberculosis on 6th March, 1848. Greatly grieved by Mimi's death, Murger nicknamed his successive girlfriends 'Mimi' in her memory.

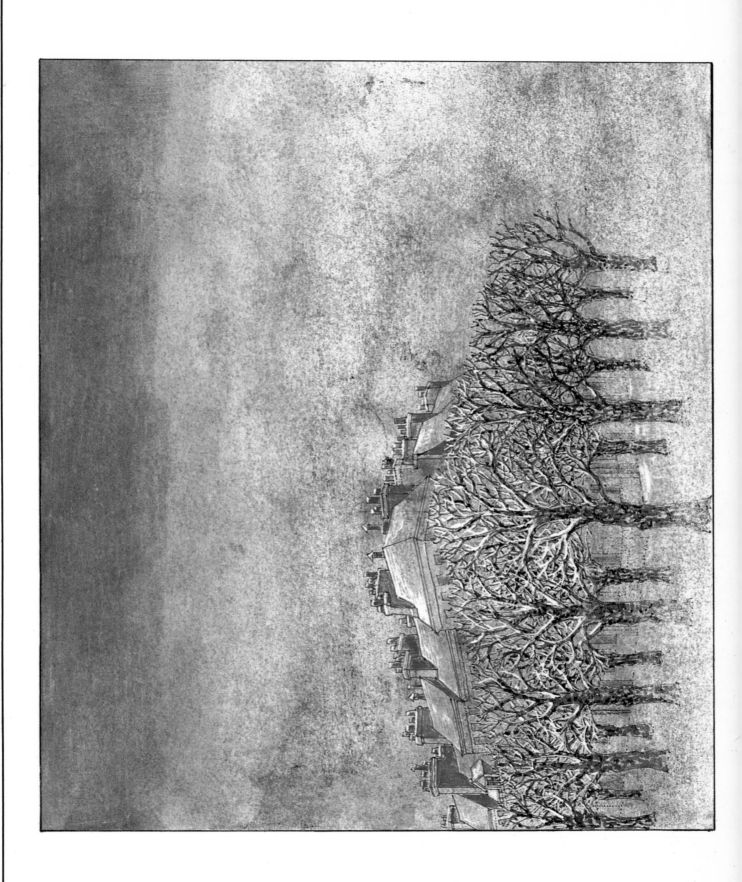

- You will see that the stage floors are covered with stretched canvas, painted to provide colour and textures to the sets, and to give an even surface for the ballet.

STAGE DIRECTIONS

N.B.: SLIDE SETS ON TO STAGE, MAKING SURE THAT THE EDGES ARE FLUSH WITH SIDES OF THEATRE.

LA BOHÈME: Backcloth for Act 1, Act 2, Act 3, Act 4.

- ACT 1: The Attic
- Slide on Attic set. Lift Tabs.
SCENE 1
Rodolpho 1c. Marcello 1a. Colline 1b.
- Place scene 1 floor in place, front of set. Position bed where shown on floor. DO NOT GLUE.
- Remove scene 1, replace by:
SCENE 2
Left to right from auditorium: Marcello, Benoit the Landlord, Schaunard, Rodolpho, Colline.
- Place scene 2 floor in place, front of set. Position bed as before. DO NOT GLUE.
- Remove scene 2, replace by:
SCENE 3
Rodolpho and Mimi.
- Place scene 3 floor in place, front of set. Position bed as before. DO NOT GLUE.

- ACT 2: In the Latin Quarter (Café Momus)
Rodolpho, Mimi, Colline, Schaunard, Marcello 9. Musetta, Alcindoro 10. Parpignol 20. Café customers; Townspeople; Street sellers; Gendarmes; Soldiers; Hawkers; Children; Servant girls etc...
- Drop Tabs, remove Act 1 set — the Attic.
- Slide on Café Momus set. Lift Tabs.
- Place scene 3 floor in place, front of set. Position bed as before. DO NOT GLUE.
- Drop Tabs, remove Act 2 set — Café Momus, Latin Quarter.

- ACT 3: The Barrière d'Enfer.
Rodolpho, Mimi 1. Marcello 2. Musetta 3. Customs officials 7, 8, 9. Tavern customers 4, 5 etc...
- Slide on Barrière d'Enfer set. Lift Tabs.
- Drop Tabs, remove Act 3 set — Barrière d'Enfer.

- ACT 4: The Attic.
Rodolpho 4a. Mimi 4b. Colline 4c. Schaunard 4d. Musetta, Marcello 4e.
- Place scene 4 floor in Attic set, front of set. Place Mimi on bed. Position bed where shown. DO NOT GLUE.
- Slide Attic set on. Lift Tabs.
- Drop Tabs at end of Act 4.

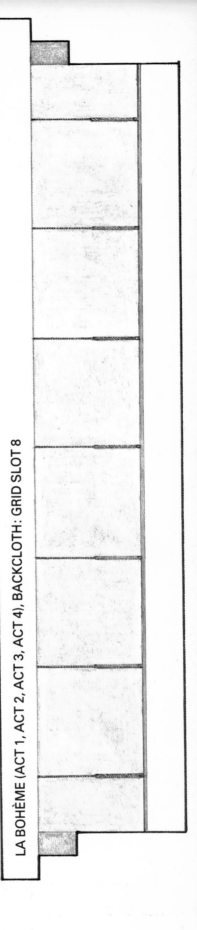

LA BOHÈME (ACT 1, ACT 2, ACT 3, ACT 4), BACKCLOTH: GRID SLOT 8

LA BOHÈME Act 1 and Act 4: The Attic

Cut out the pieces along the black lines, score and fold as shown on p. 5. Keep the pieces carefully. Before glueing make sure that the folded pieces match the shapes of the finished model on photograph. Matching glue tracks on walls, bases and stage floor have matching capital letters.

Cut attic door open. Cut out window panes.

Glue the pieces in the following alphabetical order:

- Fold and glue rostrum A, glue to stage floor A.
- Glue walls B, C, D to back of rostrum A, glue to stage floor A.
- Glue walls B, C, D to back of rostrum D and to stage floor B, C, D.
- Glue walls E, F, G, I to stage floor E, F, G, I. Fold wall E flap and glue behind wall D. Fold back chimney stacks walls and glue to back of wall D.
- Glue studio draperies and canvases to studio wall. Glue easel to rostrum.
- Glue studio zinc roof to walls D and E. Glue posts to rostrum front and beam to beam.
- Fold and glue rostrum J, glue to stage floor J.
- Glue small steps to front of rostrum A, between posts.
- Glue balustrade to rostrum J, glue band to base of balustrade.
- Fold and glue stairs K, glue to stage floor K, glue bannisters to stairs, glue band to base of bannisters, glue end of bannisters to wall.
- Glue wall L, M to stage floor L, M. Fold flaps, glue to wall. Glue draperies.
- Glue large window O to stage floor O, fold and glue sides and top flaps to wall and roof.
- Glue rostrum P (landing) to stage floor P and behind attic door wall.
- Fold and glue big roof (p. 59) in place, glueing first big flap to front of studio, then close roof like a box lid and glue to walls F, G, H, I and to roof.
- Glue house walls Q, R to stage floor Q, R. Fold and glue chimney. Glue roof.
- Glue house walls S, T to stage floor S, T. Fold flap and glue to back of wall R.
- Glue small slate roof S, T to chimney stacks wall E, front and side and to back of attic door wall.
- Glue house wall U to landing P and to stage floor U.

▲ STAGE RIGHT

- Glue remaining small zinc roof (p. 59) to wall V.
- Glue house walls V, W to stage floor V, W. Fold and glue chimney. Glue roof.
- Fold and glue braces 1, 2 and 3. Glue brace 1 to flat X, braces 2, 3 to flat Y. Glue brace 1 to flat X, braces 2, 3 to flat Y.
- Glue attic furniture where shown on photograph. EXCEPT BED and TABLE.
- Glue stove to stage floor, insert stove flue pipe into roof small slit.

STAGE LEFT ▼

53

La Bohème Act 1 and Act 4 Stage floor, hanger for La Bohème backcloth CUT OUT from this side

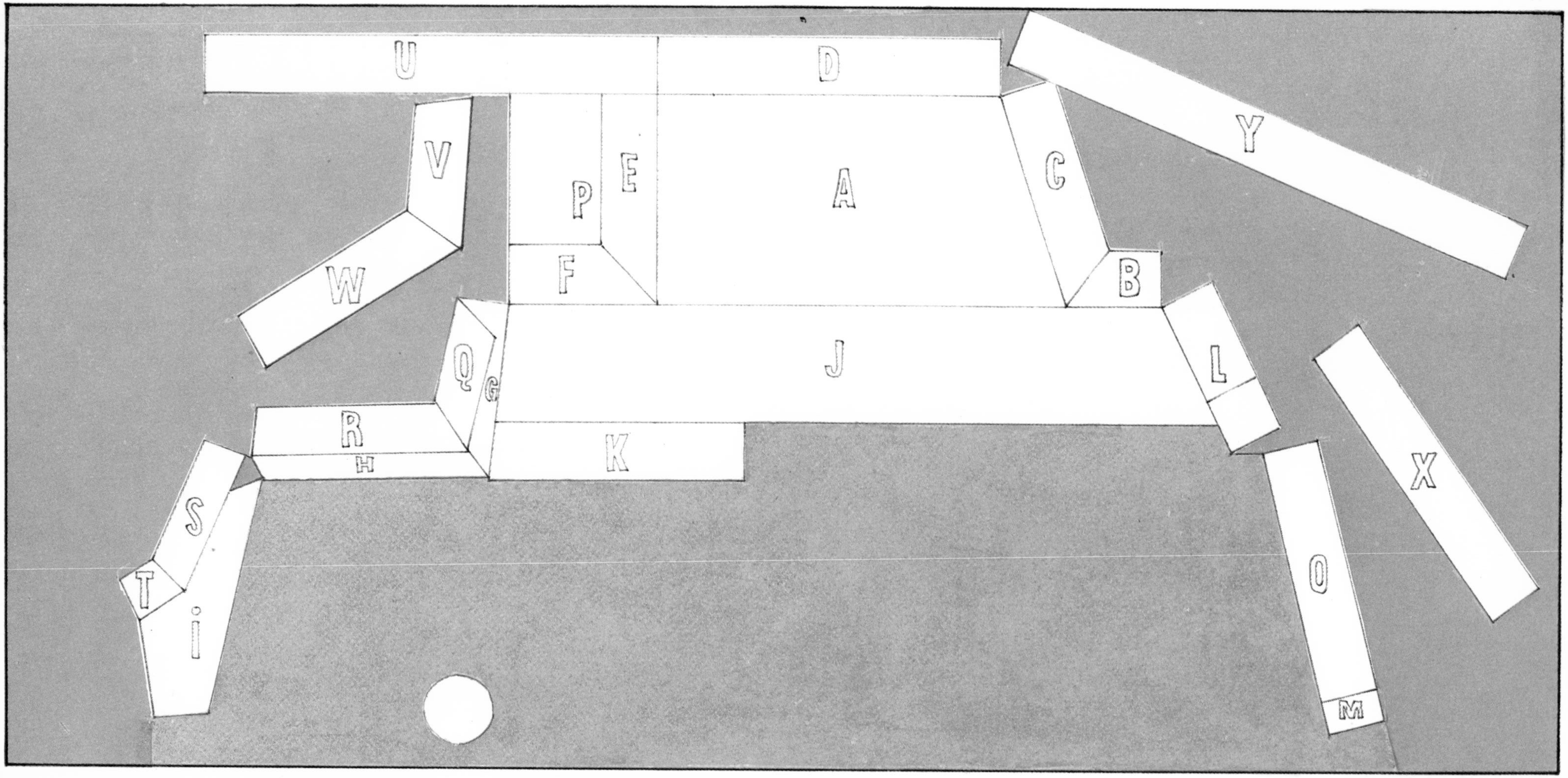

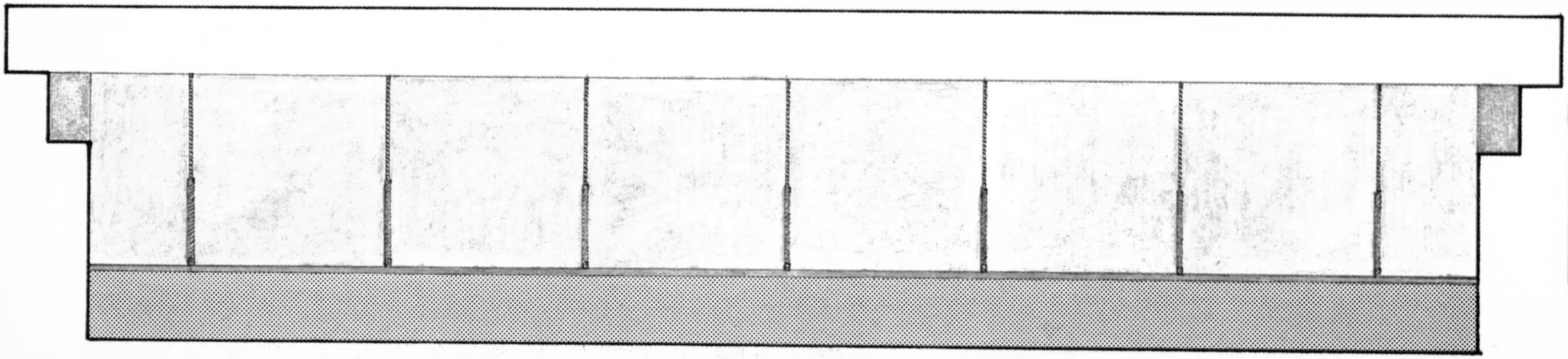

CUT OUT from this side **Act 1 and Act 4** walls; studio roof; props

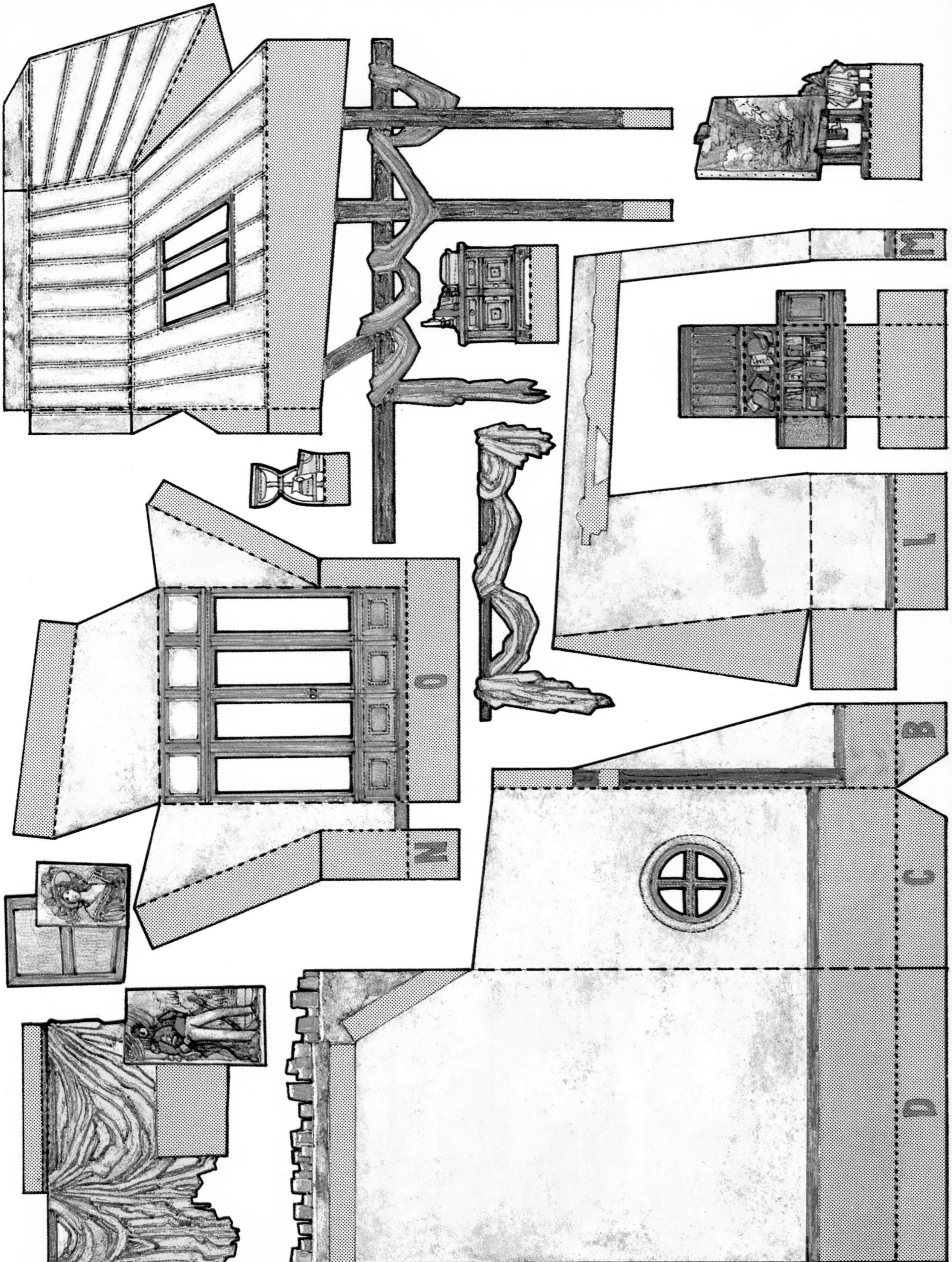

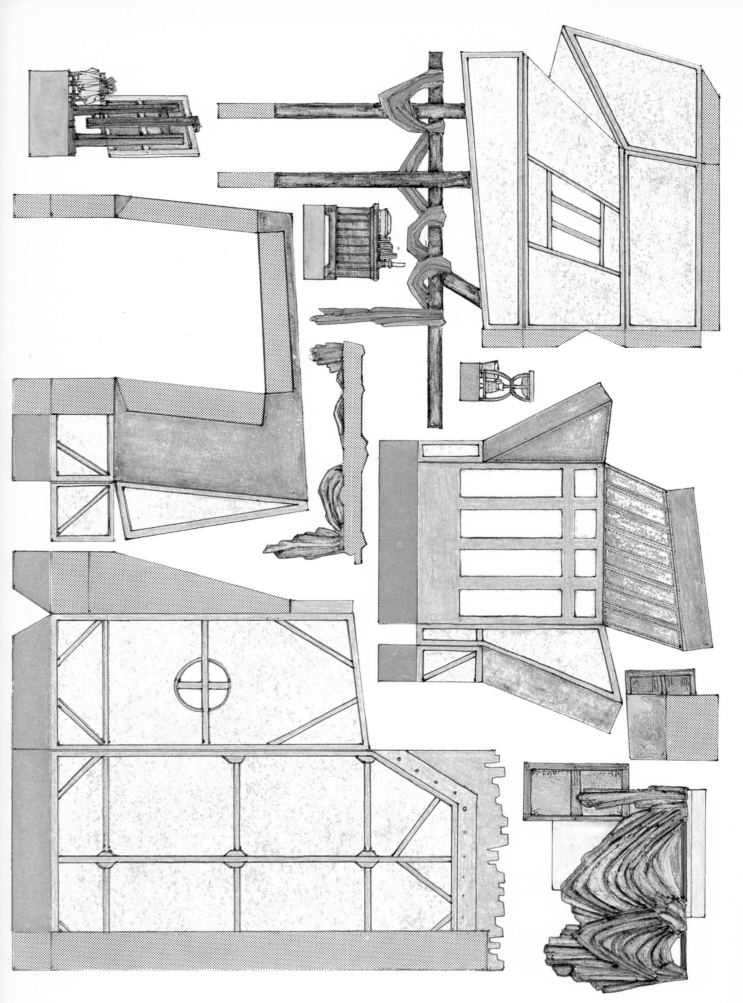

CUT OUT from this side **Act 1 and Act 4** Rostrums; balustrade; stairs and bannisters; steps; wall

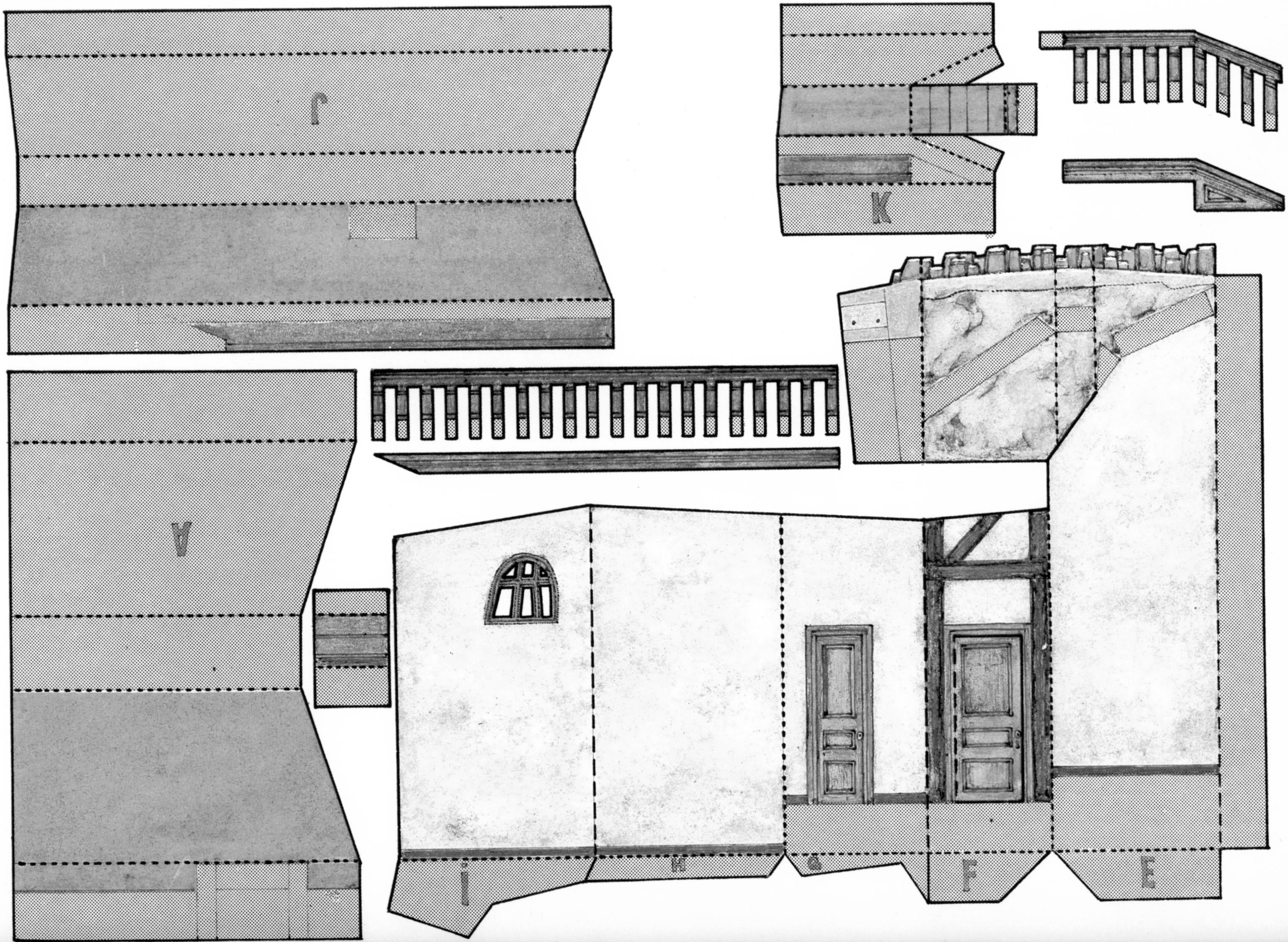

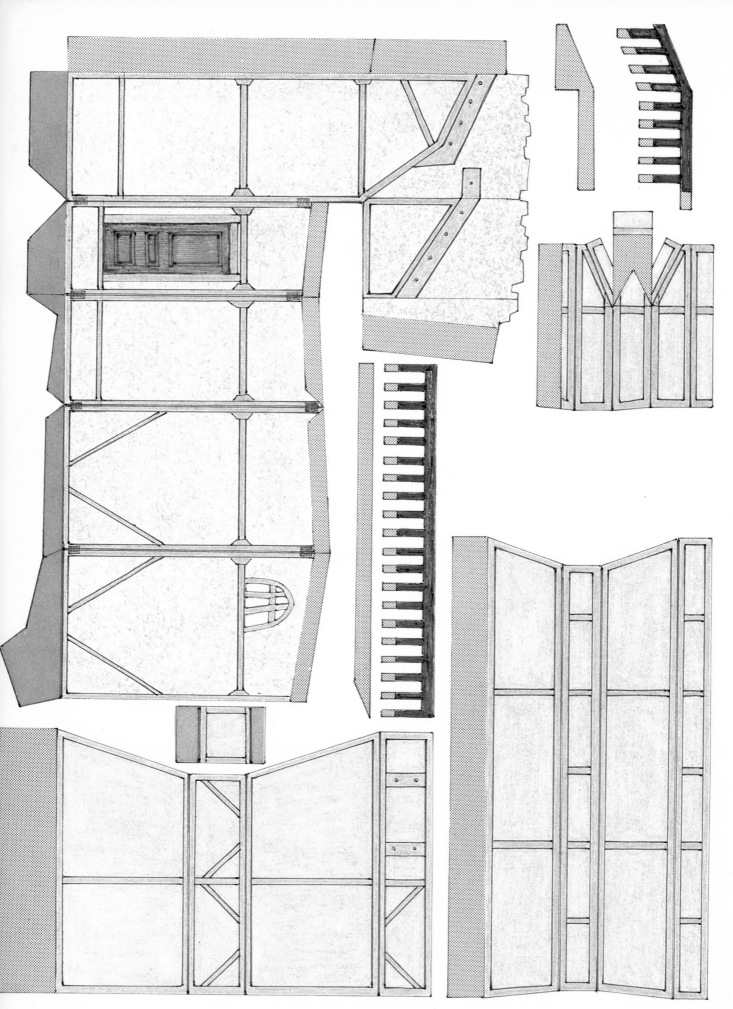

V

W

S

T

O

R

DO NOT CUT OUT from this side

X

Y

Z

1

2

3

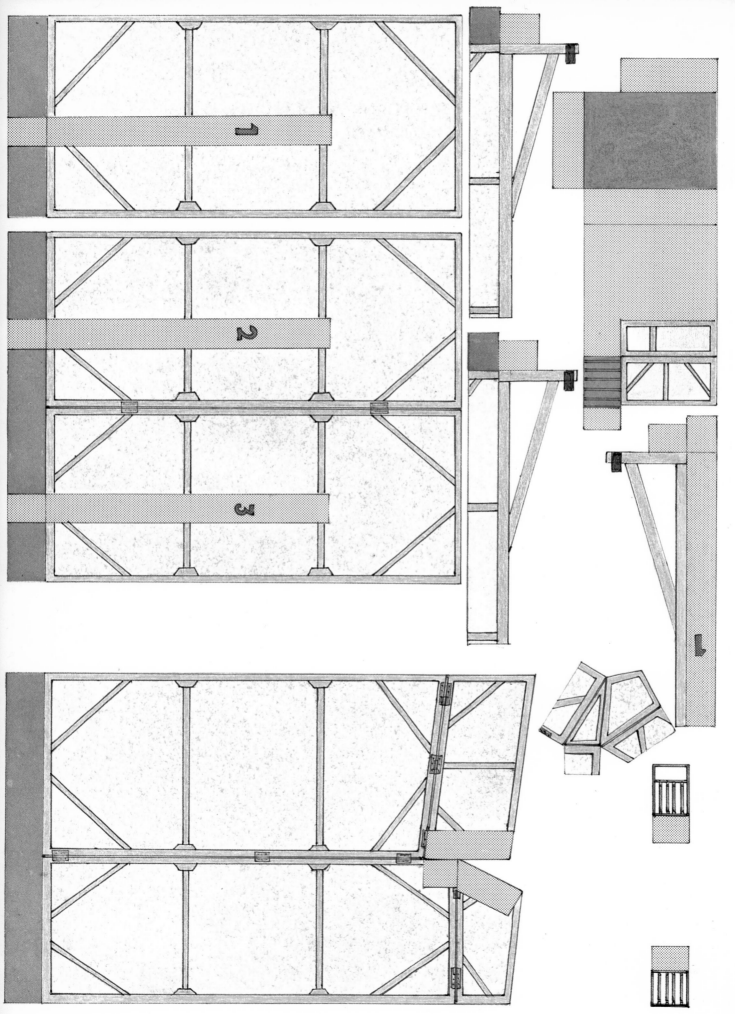

2a

2b

2c

1a

1b

1c

1d

3a

3b

3c

4a

4b

4c

4d

4e

1a

1b

1c

1d

2a

3a

3b

4a

4c

4d

4e

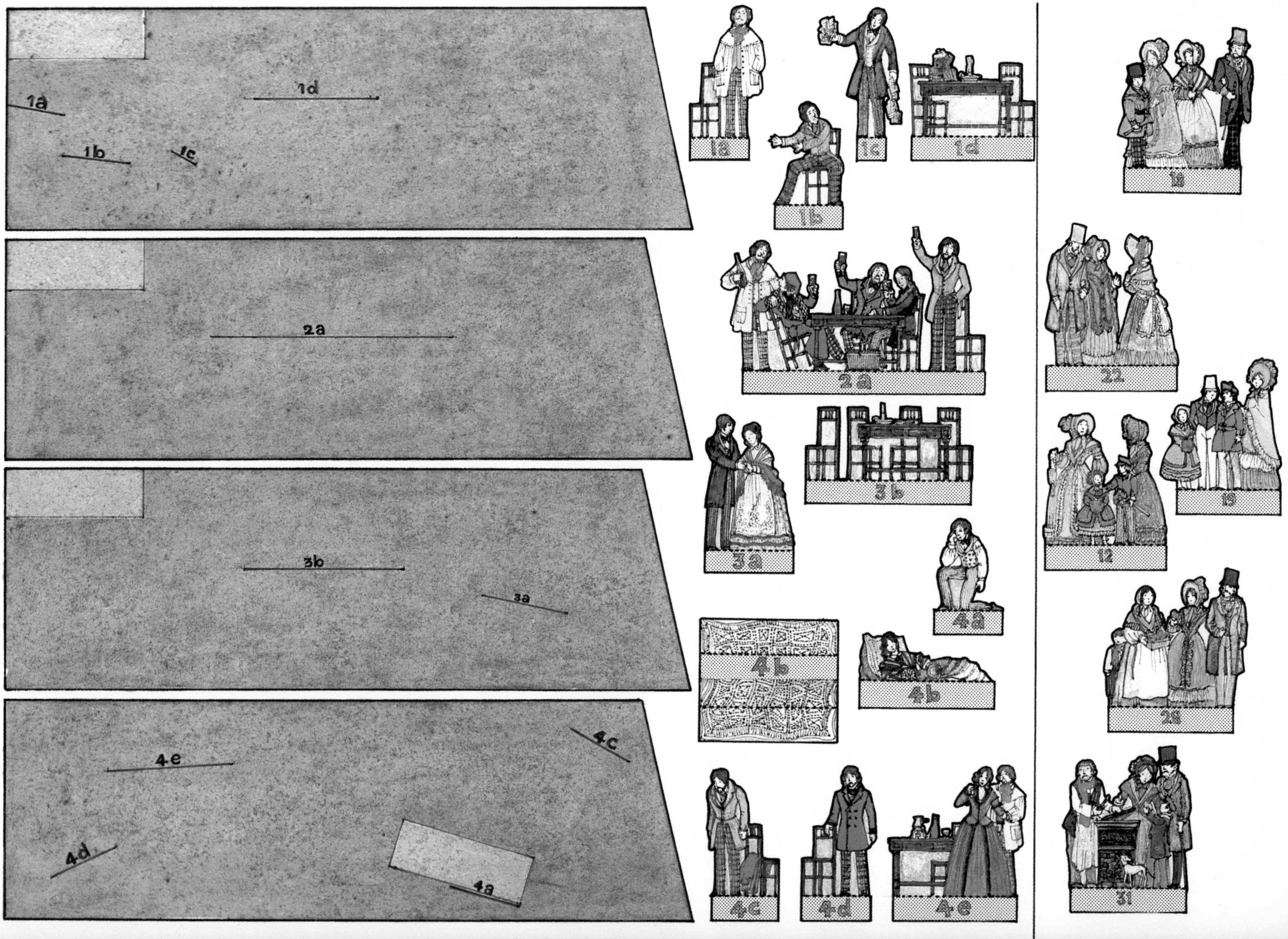

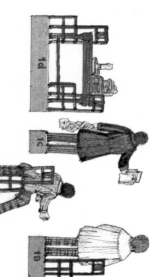

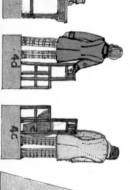

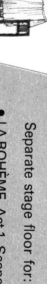

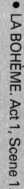

4e

4a

4d

3b

2a

1d

4c

4b

3a

1c

1b

1e

Separate stage floor for:

- LA BOHÈME. Act 1, Scene 1.

Marcello 1a. Colline 1b. Rodolpho 1c. Table 1d.
- Fold back flaps, glue along lines on this floor on top of the small matching numbers.

Separate stage floor for:

- LA BOHÈME. Act 1, Scene 2.

Marcello, Benoit the Landlord, Schaunard, Rodolpho, Colline 2a.
- Fold back flaps, glue along lines on this floor on top of the small matching numbers.

Separate stage floor for:

- LA BOHÈME. Act 1, Scene 3.

Rodolpho, Mimi 3a. Table 3b.
- Fold back flaps, glue along lines on this floor on top of the small matching numbers.

Separate stage floor for:

- LA BOHÈME. Act 4.

Rodolpho 4a. Mimi 4b. Colline 4c. Schaunard 4d. Marcello, Musetta 4e.
- Fold back flaps, glue along lines on this floor on top of the small matching numbers. Fold bed cover, glue Mimi 4b, place on top of bed for Act 4.

LA BOHÈME Act 2: In the Latin Quarter (Café Momus)

Cut out the pieces along the black lines, score and fold as shown on p. 5.

Keep the pieces carefully.

Before glueing, make sure that the folded pieces match the shapes of the finished model on the photograph.

Matching glue tracks have matching letters or numbers. Make sure the pieces are in the right position before glueing.

Cut out and fold open the Café door.
Cut out Café window panes.

Glue the pieces in the following order:

- Glue façades A, B, C, D, E.
- CAFÉ CUSTOMERS 1, 2, 3, 4, 5: fold back flaps and glue along the lines on the Café ground floor, on top of the small matching numbers.
- Fold and glue Café first floor; glue tracks a, b, c to back of Café façade a, b, c.
- Glue Café inside walls F, G to stage floor F, G; glue Café first floor tracks f, g to walls f, g.
- Glue wall F flap to back of adjoining wall D.
- CAFÉ CUSTOMERS 6, 7: fold back flaps and glue along the lines on the Café first floor, on top of the small matching numbers.
- Slot spiral staircase 8 into first floor slit, fold and glue flaps to first floor and ground floor.
- Glue wall H to stage floor H, glue first floor track h to wall h.
- Fold and glue brace 6, glue to track 6 on back of wall H and to stage floor.
- Glue façades I, J, K, L to stage floor I, J, K, L.
- Fold and glue braces 4 and 5, glue to tracks 4 and 5 behind walls I, K and to stage floor.
- SINGERS (some are also on p. 63): Fold back flaps and glue along the lines to stage floor, on top of the small matching numbers.
- Glue façades M, N, O, P, Q to stage floor M, N, O, P, Q.
- Fold and glue braces 1, 2, 3, glue to tracks 1, 2, 3 behind walls

M, O, Q and to stage floor.
- Glue Café Momus lamp to Café façade.
- Glue lanterns and flags across the streets as shown on the photograph.

▲ STAGE RIGHT

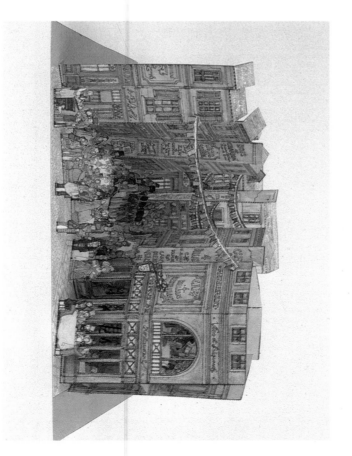

STAGE LEFT ▼

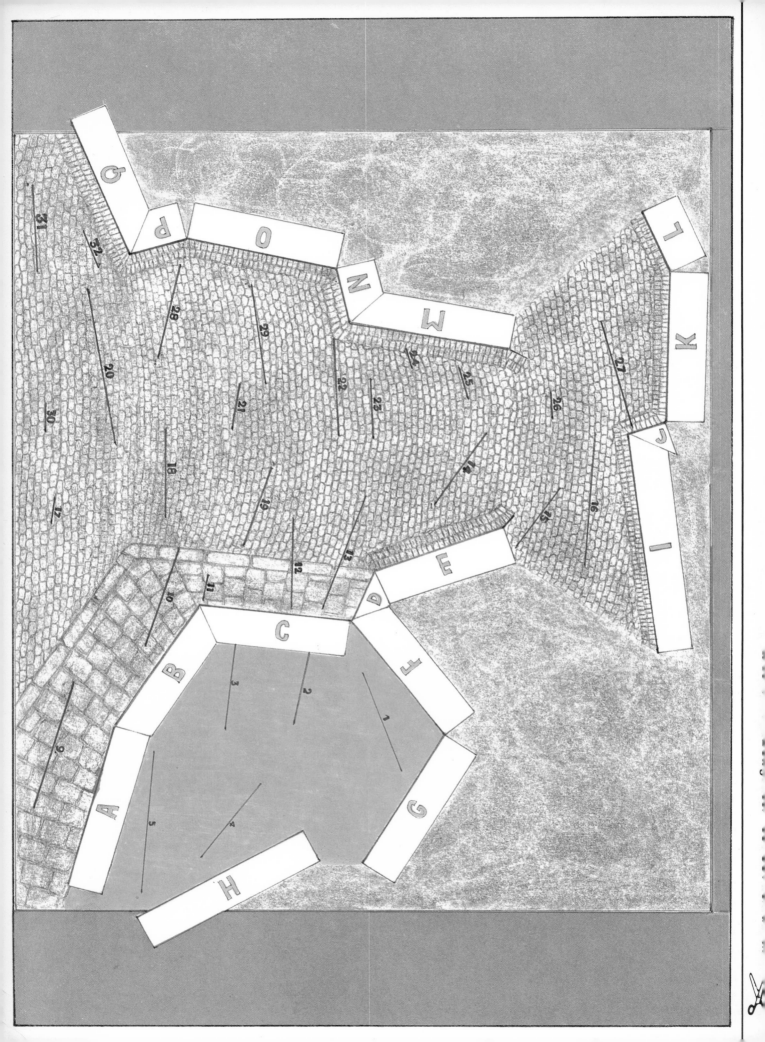

CAFÉ MOMUS 4 BILLARDS DÉ JEUNERS SOUPERS CAFÉ BIÈRE VINS et Liqueurs

CAFÉ · 4 · BILLARDS RESTAURANT

RESTAURANT · Café · Bière · Vins et Liqueurs · Restaurant · Restaurant

VENTE ET ACHAT-RÉPARATIONS · ÉCHANGE DE TOUTES SORTES

CUT OUT from this side **Act 2** Café first floor; spiral staircase; back wall; façades; lanterns; cast

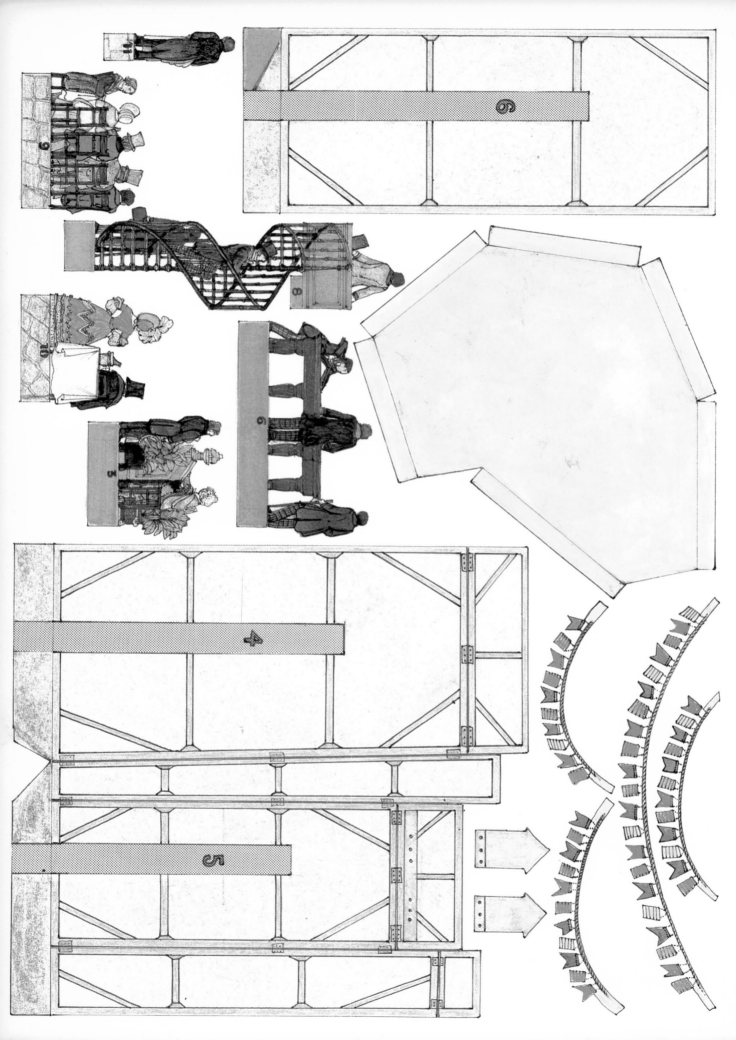

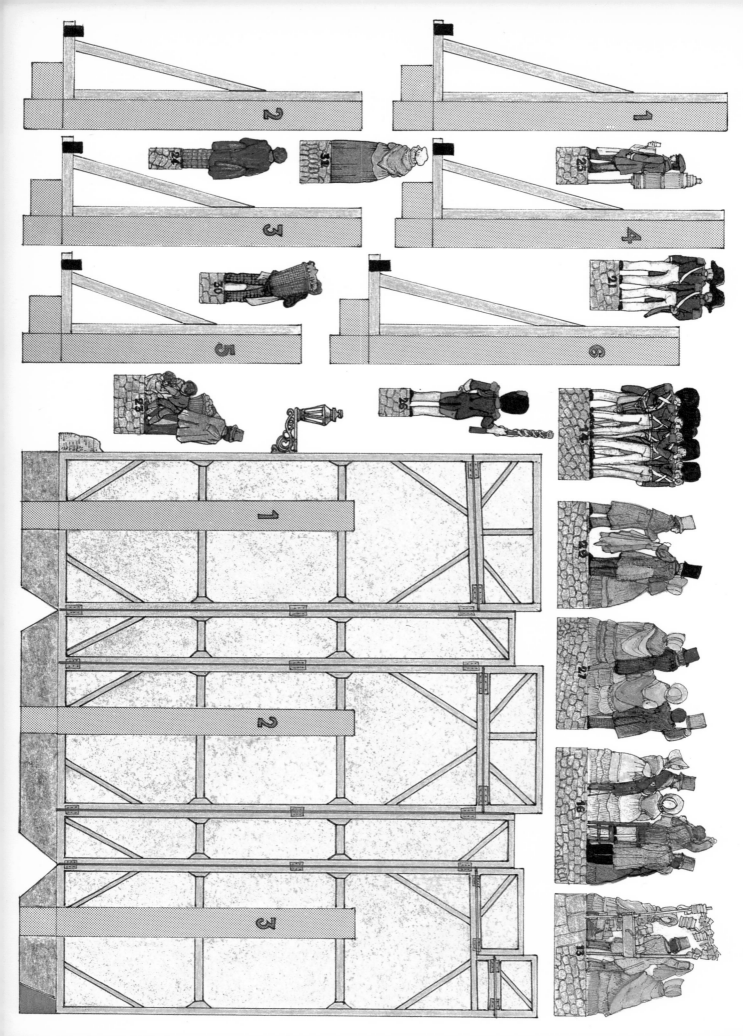

LA BOHÈME Act 3: The Barrière d'Enfer

Cut out the pieces along the black lines, score and fold as shown on p. 5.

Keep the pieces carefully.

Before glueing, make that sure the folded pieces match the shapes of the finished model on photograph.

Matching glue tracks have either matching letters, capital letters or numbers.

Make sure the pieces are in the right position before glueing.

Glue the pieces in the following order:

TAVERN
- Cut out and fold open tavern door and two opening windows.
- Fold and glue tavern façades A, B to stage floor B.
- Fold and glue tavern roof.
- Fold and glue tavern front steps, glue to stage floor C, glue railing to sides and top of steps, glue steps wall.
- Fold back small flap and glue tavern sign to tavern façade A.
- Fold and glue tavern floor a, b to back of façade walls a, b.
- Glue Stage Exit steps to stage floor D.

TAVERN CUSTOMERS 4, 5: Fold back flaps and glue along
lines on tavern floor on top of the small matching numbers.

HOUSE, FAÇADES G, H
- Fold and glue tavern back wall E: glue track e to tavern floor e; glue track E to stage floor E, tavern back wall F to stage floor F.
- Fold and glue façades G, H to stage floor G, H.
- Glue street lamp to back of façade H.
- Fold and glue roof.

HOUSE, FAÇADES I, J
- Fold and glue matching brace 1, to back of façade H and floor.
- Fold and glue façades I, J to stage floor I, J.
- Fold and glue roof.
- Fold and glue braces 1, 2 to 1, 2 back of façades and floor.
- Fold and glue tree branches 10, to 10 back of façade J.

TOLL GATE and RAILING
- Fold and glue toll gate railing K to stage floor K.
- Glue stage right end of toll gate to back of tavern back wall E.
- Fold and glue matching braces 7, 8 to 7, 8 back of toll gate and floor.

SINGERS
- Fold back flaps and glue along lines to stage floor on top of the matching small numbers.

BRAZIER, BENCHES, BARRELS
- Fold and glue on top of the matching small numbers on stage floor.

'OCTROI', FAÇADES M, L
- Fold and glue façades M, L to stage floor M, L.
- Fold and glue roof.
- Fold and glue braces 4, 5 to 4, 5 back of façades and floor.

TREES
- Fold back flaps and glue trees O, N, P to stage floor O, N, P.
- Fold back and glue small flap on tree O to tavern façade, small flap on tree N to house façade I.
- Glue tree P to 'Octroi' façade M with small dab of glue.

TREE BRANCHES
- Fold back brace and glue branches g to tavern back wall.
- Glue remaining tree branches to house façade G front of stage left so that the top of the branches is level with tree top O.

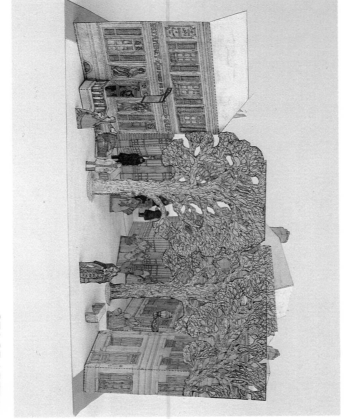

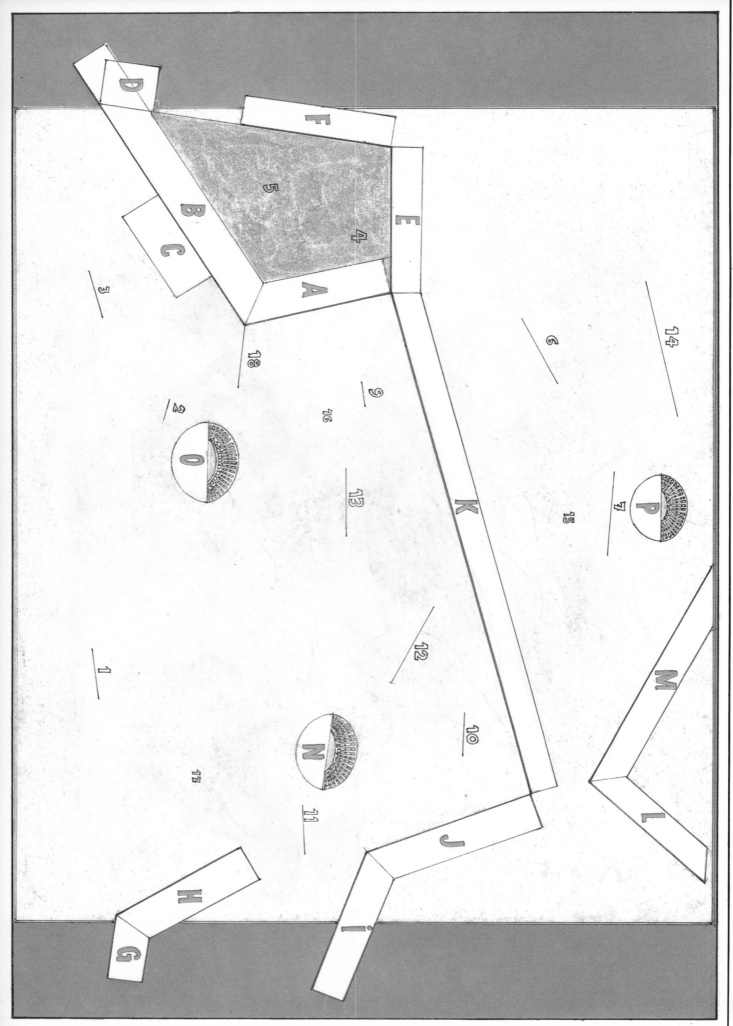

CUT OUT from this side **Act 3** Tavern façade; steps; tavern sign; façades; braces; marble benches; barrels

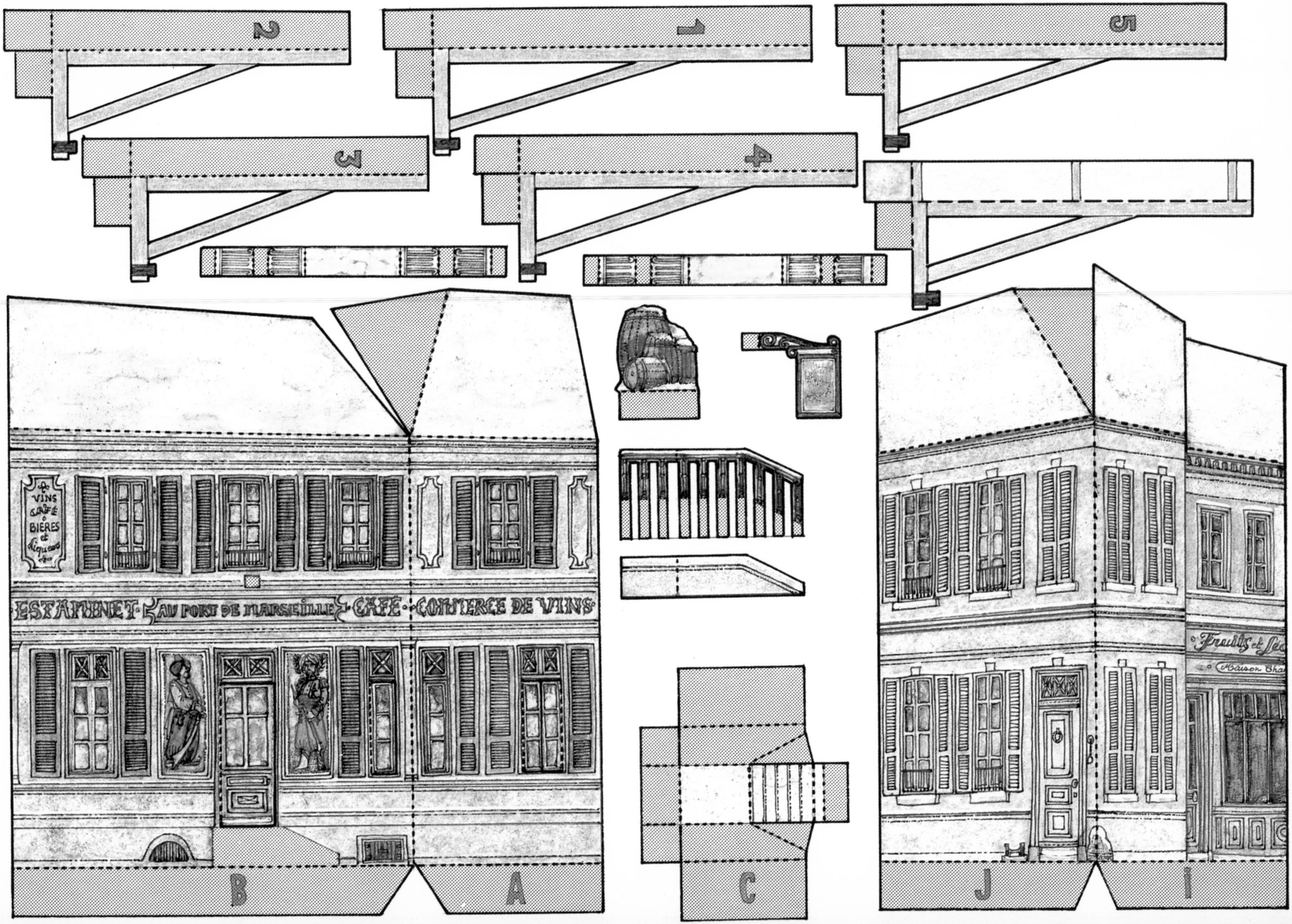
2
1
5
3
4
VINS CAFÉ BIÈRES et Liqueurs
ESTAMINET AU PORT DE MARSEILLE CAFÉ COMMERCE DE VINS
B
A
C
J
I
Fruits et Lé

DO NOT CUT OUT from this side

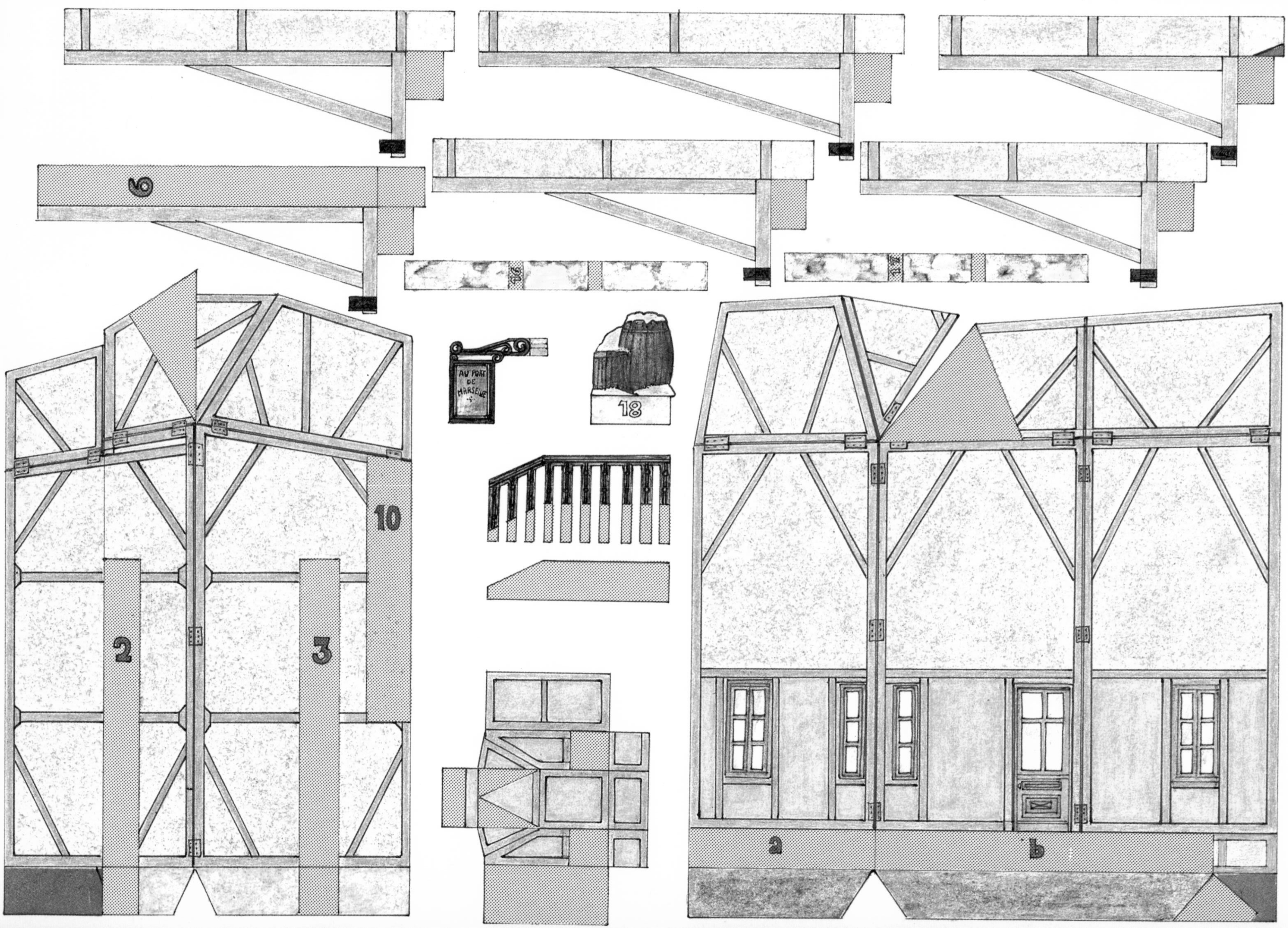

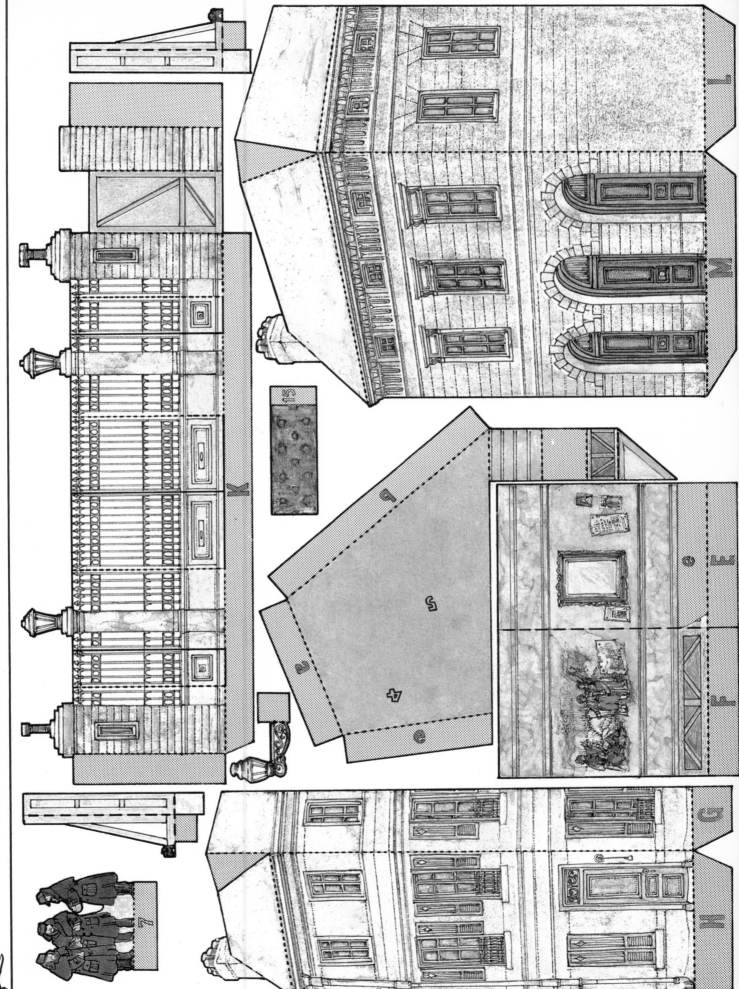

DO NOT CUT OUT from this side

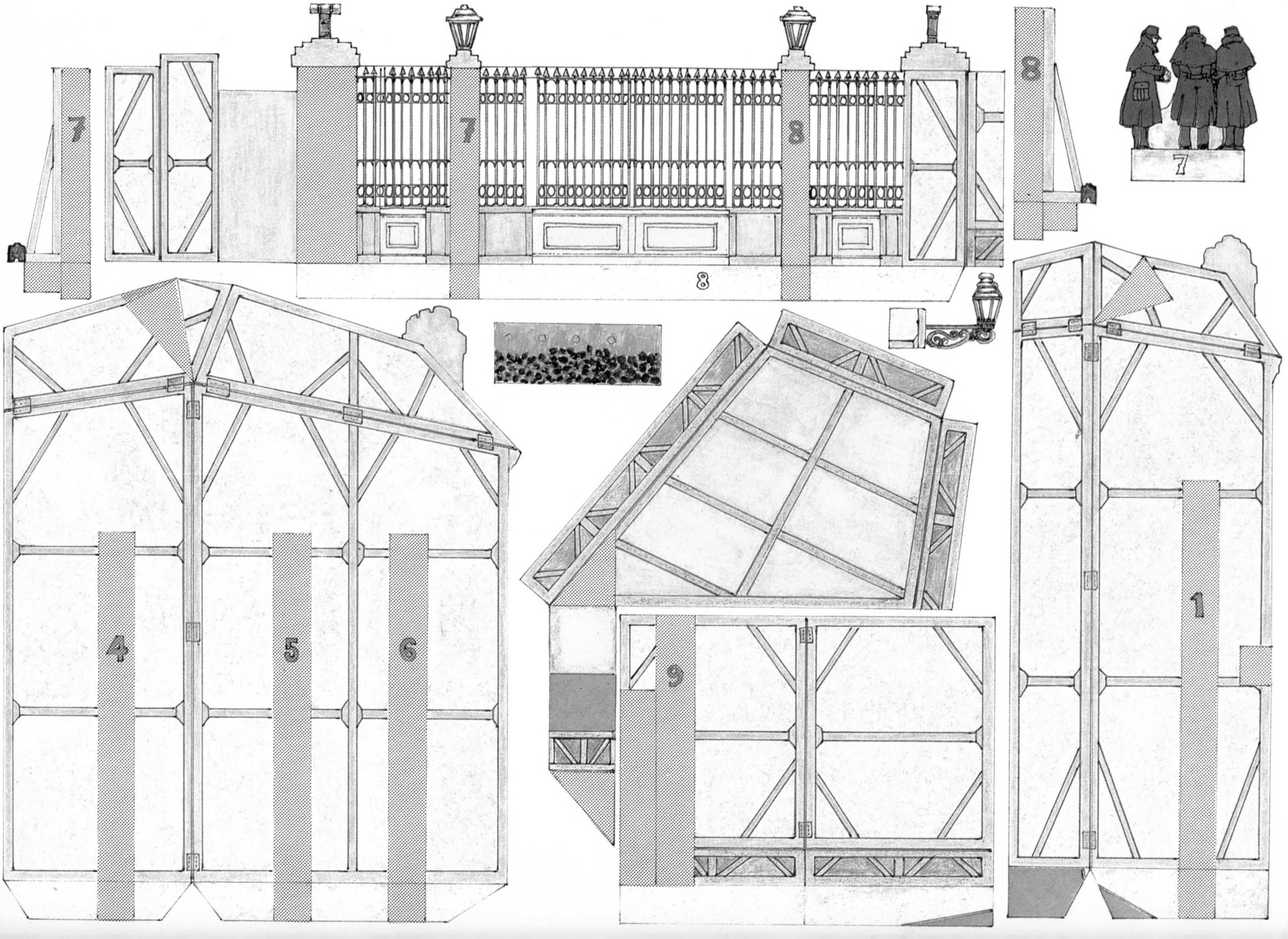

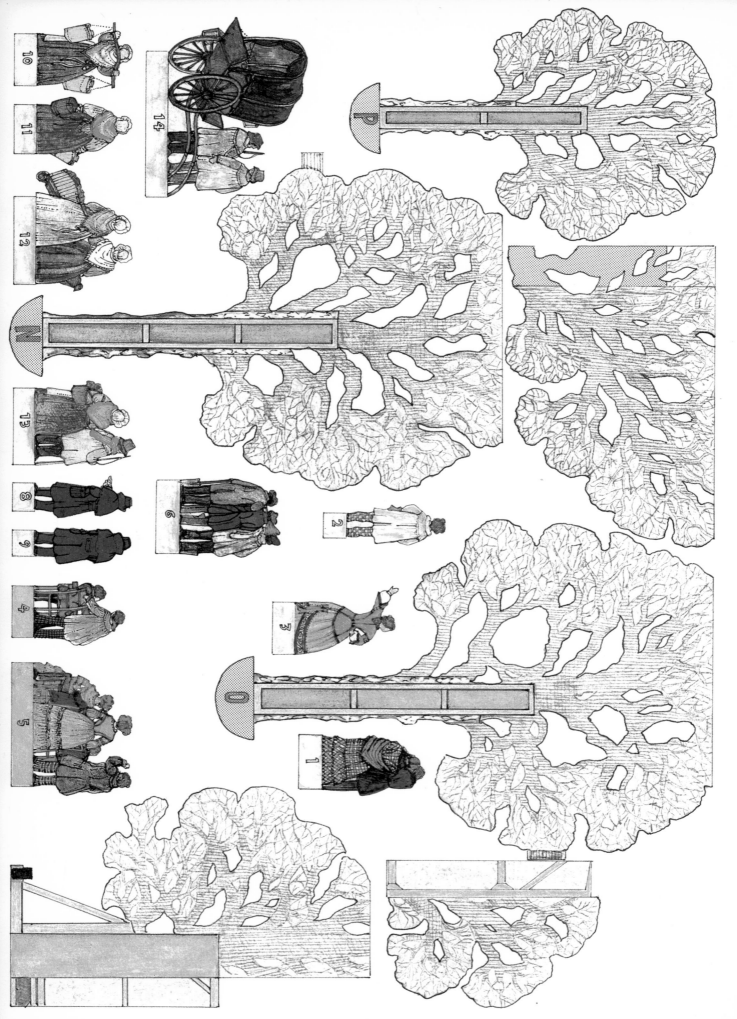

THE SLEEPING BEAUTY
Ballet in a prologue and four acts

Music by Pyotr Ilyich TCHAIKOVSKY
Choreography by Marius PETIPA

King Florestan XXIV
His Queen
Princess Aurora
Prince Florimund
Cattalabutte (Master of Ceremonies)
The Fairy Carabosse
The Lilac Fairy

Prince Florestan and his sisters
Puss-in-Boots and the White Cat
The Blue Bird and Princess Florine
Red Riding Hood and the Wolf
Beauty and the Beast
Hop-o'-my-Thumb
The Three Ivans

Prologue: The Christening

The Scene: In the Hall in the Palace of King Florestan
Time: 17th Century

It is the Christening day of the King's daughter, Princess Aurora. As they assemble for the festivities the nurse proudly shows off the baby to the delighted courtiers.

Cattalabutte, the royal Master of Ceremonies, gives orders for the final preparations. He scans the list of guests who have been invited. Has anyone been forgotten? No, it is complete! Satisfied, he bows deeply as trumpets announce the arrival of the King and Queen. The Queen kisses her baby and greets the courtiers whilst the King confers with Cattalabutte.

The Princess Aurora's six Fairy Godmothers enter the Hall accompanied by their cavaliers and small pages who carry on silk cushions the gifts each of the fairies has chosen for her Godchild. The Lilac Fairy leads the group who lean tenderly over the cradle to give their blessings to the tiny Princess. Then one by one the Fairy Godmothers dance for the Royal Family and the court.

First, the Fairy of the Crystal Fountain, as light and softly graceful as her name; her dance suggests falling drops of plashing water. Then the Fairy of the Enchanted Garden, whose quick steps and accelerating pirouettes follow the happy tempo of the music with the brightness of a summer's day.

The Fairy of the Woodland Glades advances with precise, elegant steps to a pizzicato, followed by rapid, brilliant dancing. The flash of a yellow costume announces the Fairy of the Song Birds whose dance is like the flutter of wings as she flickers across the stage. Next, the Fairy of the Golden Vine whose movements are short, quick and sharp. She turns her head pointing the index fingers of both hands faster and faster with the staccato music until she whirls to a stop. Lastly, with the slow serene rhythm of the waltz, the Lilac Fairy comes forward to dance with a gently flowing line and regal authority.

The six Fairy Godmothers dance with their cavaliers and then present their magic gifts to the King and Queen — all except the Lilac Fairy, for just as she is about to do so, there is a sudden rumbling of thunder, and a flash of lightning.

The King is worried, and the Queen anxious for the safety of her baby. A page helplessly points to the archway of the Palace entrance; someone evil is approaching. The King rushes to Cattalabutte, and snatching the guest list from him scans it rapidly; to his horror he realises that one name has been omitted. As the courtiers cower in terror two great rats dart in menacingly to reconnoitre the scene. They scuttle out again, only to return with more rats dragging the hideous coach in which the wicked Fairy Carabosse is seated. The coach circles the stage in a wide arc, sweeping the terrified courtiers aside. Furious, Carabosse climbs down from her coach and demands to know why she has not been invited to the Christening. The King blames the forgetful Cattalabutte saying that he is the real culprit. Carabosse contemptuously berates the Master of Ceremonies as he kneels quivering at her feet, begging for mercy. But the wicked fairy is full of malice and vengeance. With her evil retinue she performs a dance of spiteful hate, then turning towards the cradle she suddenly points her finger. 'The baby Aurora,' she promises, 'will grow up to be the most beautiful Princess in the world — then on her twentieth birthday she will prick her finger on a spindle — and die!' Throwing back her head and laughing triumphantly she approaches to curse the child. But the Lilac Fairy steps out from behind the cradle to keep her away, and the other fairies gather round to protect the infant from harm.

The sneering Carabosse, unable to overcome the Lilac Fairy, climbs back into her coach and, shaking her fist at the King and court, is drawn away by her servile rats.

The distraught Queen sobs as the King, appalled, tries to comfort her. But the Lilac Fairy has not yet bestowed her gift on the Princess; although she cannot lift the curse of Carabosse she can still save the Princess's life.

Coming forward the Lilac Fairy tells the desperate parents that their daughter will indeed grow up to be beautiful, and will prick her finger as foretold, but she

will not die. Instead, she and the entire court will sleep for a hundred years. One day a handsome Prince will come, and he will fall in love with her. He will kiss her and she will awake. Then everyone will live happily ever after.

The King and Queen are greatly pleased and thank the Lilac Fairy, and the court and fairies rejoice as the curtain falls.

ACT 1: The Spell

The Scene: In the Garden of the Palace twenty years later
Time: 17th Century

Villagers and courtiers are assembled to celebrate Princess Aurora's twentieth birthday. As the Lilac Fairy and Carabosse predicted she has now grown into a beautiful young woman and four Princes from foreign lands have come to pay court to her.

Ever fearful of the dreadful curse of Carabosse, the King has commanded that all sharp objects must be banned from the kingdom; thus for twenty years the Princess has been free from danger.

Whilst he arranges the birthday celebrations, Cattalabutte discovers three old knitting women and, seizing their needles, threatens them with punishment. Just then the King and Queen arrive. Seeing the needles the King angrily condemns the old women to death, but the Queen implores him to pardon them, reminding him that it is Aurora's birthday. The King smiles his forgiveness.

Village girls carrying hoops garlanded with flowers run in to dance a waltz, weaving in and out under the garlands around the stage in circles. They are followed by eight of Aurora's friends — four girls carrying mandolins and four with roses — and then to a joyous burst of music the young Princess herself appears in the garden in a series of gay leaps and bounds, dancing with exuberant happiness.

The Queen embraces her daughter and the King kisses her forehead before introducing her to her four suitors: an English Prince, a Spanish Prince, an Indian Prince and a French Prince. In the famous 'Rose Adagio' Aurora dances with each of her suitors in turn. As the first Prince takes her hand he walks round her in a circle as she turns on one point, releasing her hand as the next Prince steps forward to take it. The Princes offer her roses which she gathers into a bouquet and gives to her mother, and Aurora dances first with one of the Princes, then on her own. Then, kneeling at her feet her suitors offer more roses; Aurora, spinning in the same number of pirouettes as there are flowers, gathers them from their outstretched hands.

The music rises to a crescendo as Aurora, her left arm lifted and balancing her body on one point, gives her right hand to each Prince in turn, lifting it to stand unsupported before the next suitor comes forward to take her hand. Finally, the last Prince releases the Princess and, poised like a fragile statue, Aurora stands motionless until the last chord of music before merrily running off into the garden. As Aurora dances joyfully with her eight friends an old hunchbacked woman, a dark hood concealing her face, mingles stealthily in the crowd. When the happy Princess dances near to her, the old woman produces a gift from the folds of her cloak — a spindle!

Barely stopping her dance, the delighted Aurora takes the spindle and begins to play with it. Rising in terror, the King warns the court of the danger and everyone tries to take the spindle from her. Too late, for the Princess Aurora has already pricked her finger. Her parents rush to her side as she shows them the wound. Seeing her father's anxious face she consoles him and comforts her worried mother. To prove to them that she is unhurt she begins to dance once more, but as she dances she grows dizzier, her head spins and her body grows weak and faint ... there is a clap of thunder and the Princess collapses lifeless.

The old crone steps forward, and throws back her hood. It is Carabosse who has returned to fulfil her curse. With a peal of demonic laughter, she runs from the garden as the courtiers, drawing their swords, rush after her.

A trumpet sounds, then the harp, and the Lilac Fairy returns as promised, to tell her unhappy parents that the Princess is not dead, she will merely sleep for a hundred years.

Gratefully, the King and Queen thank the good fairy, and follow as the four Princes take up the sleeping Aurora and carry her into the Palace.

The Lilac Fairy casts her spell; obedient to her command, one by one the remaining courtiers fall into a deep slumber. The garden darkens and from the ground spring shrubs and trees, rising slowly towards the sky to enfold and entwine the garden and Palace, hiding them from sight for a century of sleep.

ACT 2: The Vision

The Scene: A clearing in the forest 100 years later
Time: 18th Century

Prince Florimund is out hunting wild boar with his court — dukes, duchesses, marchionesses and marquesses. The Prince's old aide Gallison totters exhausted into the clearing followed shortly by Prince Florimund who bows to the courtiers. The assembled company drink wine from gold goblets, and amidst the revelry a high-spirited countess suggests a game of 'blindman's buff'. She binds Gallison's eyes, and the old man — who has drunk too much wine — chases after the courtiers, who further tease him by spinning him around and whipping at his feet with their riding crops.

Stumbling around dizzily, Gallison eagerly takes the hand of someone whom he imagines to be a charming lady. Removing his blindfold he finds himself, to his great astonishment, embracing a man.

The Countess persuades Prince Florimund to dance a mazurka with her, and the courtiers join in with swishing whips.

Peasant boys and girls enter and dance a farandole, holding hands as they curve about the stage in a serpentine line.

The sound of hunting horns announces the arrival of beaters who have sighted a wild boar. The Prince, his thoughts elsewhere, has grown tired of games and dances. He urges the hunting party to go after the beast whilst he remains in the clearing.

Left alone, the Prince watches night fall. As the moon rises he feels sad and full of strange melancholy. He gazes out over the lake in the hope that the beautiful scene will gladden his heart. Turning away dejected, he is at first unaware of the magical boat of the Lilac Fairy, as it floats quietly into view. She is his Godmother, and knowing the cause of his deep unhappiness has appeared to answer his dreams.

The Lilac Fairy tells Prince Florimund that in a palace not far from the forest, sleeps a beautiful princess. This lovely girl is bewitched by a spell and has slept for a hundred years. She will sleep forever unless a handsome prince falls in love with her. His kiss will awaken her. The Prince is fascinated, but a little sceptical, and asks the Lilac Fairy to show him the princess.

At the fairy's command Princess Aurora appears in a vision surrounded by forest nymphs and dances with Florimund before vanishing away into the night.

The Prince, who has fallen in love with this vision of Aurora, begs the Lilac Fairy to take him to where he can find her. Together they set sail across the lake towards King Florestan's Palace.

ACT 3: The Awakening

The Scene: The Palace Gates and Princess Aurora's Bedchamber

Arriving at the far side of the lake, Prince Florimund and the Lilac Fairy disembark and enter the Enchanted Forest. The Lilac Fairy guides the astonished Prince through enormous, gnarled, twisted trees and thick, tangled undergrowth. Carabosse, lurking in wait, tries to prevent them from reaching the Princess but her furious rage and threats are powerless. At last the Lilac Fairy and the Prince come to the Palace gates, half-hidden in a dense thicket of thorns.

In amazement, Florimund follows the Lilac Fairy as she leads him through the cobweb-festooned, dusty rooms and chambers of the Palace past the slumbering guards and courtiers.

In the dim light they reach the bedchamber where Princess Aurora lies sleeping. Florimund hesitates, hardly daring to disturb her. The Lilac Fairy motions him forward, he steps towards the bed, and bending towards her lovely face, kisses her softly.

The Princess Aurora stirs, opens her eyes and awakening in delighted surprise looks with adoration at the Prince who has at last released her from the spell. She rises slowly from her bed.

Prince Florimund happily gathers her in his arms and immediately the misty veil of dust and cobwebs dissolves. The dim room is flooded with light, banishing every vestige of the long night of a hundred years of sleep.

The courtiers wake too, and stretch, rubbing their eyes. The joyful King and Queen enter the bedchamber to give their blessing to their daughter and her Prince Florimund.

ACT 4: The Wedding

The Scene: The draped and decorated Hall in the Palace of King Florestan

It is the wedding day of Prince Florimund and Princess Aurora. The Master of Ceremonies Cattalabutte enters with his customary pomp and flourish, as he struts around importantly, once more arranging the festivities.

The King and Queen enter and Cattalabutte, bowing low, escorts them to the dais and signals that the dancing may begin.

Courtiers and ladies-in-waiting dance and promenade round the Hall to the strong rhythms of the polonaise.

The special guests arrive: these are fairytale characters whom the King has invited to his daughter's wedding, and they have come to pay their respects.

Aurora's brother, the Crown Prince Florestan, and their two sisters dance a lilting waltz followed by a quick, light, youthful series of steps and jumps.

The music changes its mood to the sound of mewing, sudden spits and insinuating feline movements as the White Cat and her possessive partner Puss-in-Boots begin to dance. The White Cat pretends to resist the persistent caresses of Puss, though she really enjoys them, until Puss-in-Boots can stand her teasing no longer, and carries her off, still faintly protesting.

The next of the fairytale characters, the enchanted Princess Florine and the Bluebird, perform a dazzling duet. The Bluebird and Florine cross the stage, apparently caught in soaring flight as their arms and feet beat like birds' wings.

Little Red Riding Hood tries in vain to escape the wicked Wolf, but he hides and just as she passes, catches her. Then, throwing her kicking and struggling over his shoulder, the Wolf runs off.

Three more storybook guests arrive, and first the Beast kneels imploringly at Beauty's feet, before Hop-o'-my-Thumb shows off his dancing skills with amazing leaps and bounds.

Now comes the moment everyone has been waiting for as Princess Aurora, radiant and beautiful in her wedding dress, enters with Prince Florimund.

The lords and ladies bow low and their Princess dances. The gay abandon of her youth is replaced, now that she is to be married, with a graceful elegance which reflects the nobility of her love.

The Prince holds her high above the ground showing her full loveliness to the admiring court, before he too dances a sweeping solo full of passionate, heroic splendour.

As their dance ends, the Princess Aurora turns on one point with incredible speed and then falls forward in the 'fish dive' across the Prince's bended knee. Head down near the ground, feet high above his shoulder, she is wedged between the Prince's knee and arm and supported only by the arch of her back, as the Prince opens his arms wide.

This mood of tenderness and triumph is broken when the three Ivans stomp on in a wild, whirling cossack dance.

Aurora returns once more to say farewell to her parents; she will soon go away with her Prince. Though saddened by the thought that their Princess will be leaving them, the court shares in her great happiness, and after the Polish dancers have performed a dashing and spirited mazurka, the nobles, bride and groom join in the dance and merrymaking.

The Lilac Fairy, Godmother to both Prince Florimund and Princess Aurora, appears now with her fairy attendants to give her blessing to the young couple. For the Prince and Princess, standing together in close embrace, have finally become part of a fairytale that ends happily ever after.

BIOGRAPHICAL NOTES

Pyotr Ilyich Tchaikovsky was born in 1840 in Votinsk, Russia. Although he started to play the piano at the age of seven, he went on to study law at St Petersburg. Music, however, was the stronger passion and at the age of twenty-three he gave up his official position in the Civil Service in order to study music — in great poverty — at the St Petersburg Conservatoire.

His professor, Anton Rubinstein, was a great pianist and composer who gave the young man practical and moral support; Tchaikovsky eventually became Professor of Music at Moscow Conservatoire.

A wealthy widow, Nadezhda von Meck, recognised his enormous talent and helped him financially for thirteen years by means of a yearly grant. Though they never met, but wrote letters continuously to each other, Madame von Meck even entertained Tchaikovsky lavishly on her country estate — in her absence.

A deeply melancholic young man, Tchaikovsky's life was scarred by a disastrous marriage to a young music student which broke up after only eleven weeks and developed his already morbid outlook into one of despair. Warm, shy and sensitive, his feelings were expressed intensely in the sensuous fund of his melodies which, although full of Russian sensitivity and excitement, contain no national aspirations.

Tchaikovsky's prodigious output of operas, symphonies and concertos ensured him a place in musical history, and his ballet music brought new dignity and stature to this very particular art form. He was the first late nineteenth-century Russian composer to treat the subject with respect. When, intending criticism, some of the passages in his fourth symphony were described as sounding like ballet music, Tchaikovsky retorted, 'I simply cannot see why the term should be associated with something reprehensible. There is such a thing as good ballet music'.

We can only agree, when, many years later, we listen to the eternally beautiful scores from *Swan Lake, Nutcracker* and *The Sleeping Beauty*. Writing in 1949, Sacheverell Sitwell said: 'I would go every night to see and hear *The Sleeping Beauty*. I want to listen to that sparkling score and become drugged with the immortal music. I want to admire the scenery and watch the glittering dancers. And go again tomorrow afternoon and evening.'

Tchaikovsky died in 1893. Despite the warnings of

friends, he drank unboiled water and died within a week of cholera.

Victor Marius Alphonse Petipa was born in Marseilles in 1818 or 1822. We cannot be sure of the exact date as his own account does not tally with the date on his birth certificate. He was descended from Mademoiselle Petit-pas, principal dancer at the Paris Opéra. His father, Jean Antoine, was a dancer and his mother an actress. They had five children of whom four followed theatrical careers. His brother Lucien became a well-known dancer at the Paris Opéra. Shortly after Marius's birth his father became principal dancer and ballet-master of the Théâtre de la Monnaie in Brussels, until the 1830 Revolution put a stop to theatrical performances. The family moved to Antwerp where Jean Antoine Petipa leased a theatre, but they made no money and the financial situation soon became desperate.

The Petipa family returned to Brussels where they spent several years before moving to Bordeaux. It was here that Marius started to study dancing and choreography with serious determination, and soon obtained a post in Nantes as principal dancer and ballet-master. He staged three ballets for this tiny company, then he broke a leg during rehearsal; the director of the theatre refused to pay him unless he was dancing, so Petipa promptly arranged a Spanish dance in which he appeared seated playing the castanets, whilst the ballerina danced alone.

Leaving Nantes, Marius and his father Jean Antoine set sail for New York. They met with disaster. Father as ballet-master and son as premier dancer had been promised a fortune by an impresario called Lecomte. Their first performance on arrival was a play which included a ballet. For the opening week they received a small advance of money, but attendances dwindled and they were paid only half their salaries. The second, third and fourth week produced no money at all; this state of affairs, coupled with an outbreak of yellow fever in New York, persuaded father and son to return to France. Marius noted ruefully, 'Our acquaintance with the States turned out to be sad'.

Back in Paris, Marius joined the class of Auguste Vestris. Although he never shared the success of his brother Lucien, he danced with Carlotta Grisi in 1840. Invited back to Bordeaux where he became premier dancer, he was allowed to stage four ballets.

In 1843 Marius went to the King's Theatre in Madrid where in a Tyrolean character dance he kissed his partner. It was forbidden to kiss on the stage in Spain at that time, so he was arrested. An affair with a beautiful Spanish girl got him into more trouble, for he had a rival for her affections, in the person of the First Secretary at the French Embassy. This resulted in a duel during which his opponent's pistol misfired and Marius' bullet fractured the diplomat's jaw. This adventure had two expected results: full houses — and Petipa was forced to leave Spain!

Returning to Paris he danced a pas de quatre at the Opéra with his brother Lucien and the two Elssler sisters, Fanny and Theresa. Shortly after this Marius Petipa received a letter from the ballet-master at the Maryinski Theatre, St Petersburg, offering him a salary of 10,000 francs. He arrived in St Petersburg on 24th May, 1847.

For his début at the Maryinski Theatre Marius Petipa mounted the French ballet *Paquita*, dancing the role of Count d'Hervilly.

Petipa was successful largely through the strength of his acting and character dancing and, though not perfect for 'danseur noble roles', he was a reliable partner for the ballerina, and also had an imposing stage presence.

Petipa continued to compose small works — mainly for his first wife Maria — while at the same time staging other people's ballets and assisting the ballet-master. His first success came with the five-act ballet *Pharaoh's Daughter*, which he completed in a rehearsal time of six weeks. The spectacular ensembles and dramatic ballerina role were immensely popular and Petipa was appointed as one of the company's ballet-masters.

Seven years later, in 1862, he was promoted to take entire charge of the company. His contract specified that he must create one major work each season, and Petipa produced a long succession of magnificent ballets in a career spanning over sixty years. To name here but a few: *Don Quixote* 1869, *La Bayadère* 1877, *The Sleeping Beauty* 1890, *Swan Lake* 1895 (jointly with Ivanov three years after Tchaikovsky's death) and *Raymonda* 1898. Petipa not only created new ballets but he also improved and added to others, such as *Giselle*.

In his bad Russian (he never learnt to speak the language in spite of the many years he spent in the country), Petipa explained his ideas to the dancers, having prepared everything in advance. By the use of mime coupled with a few Russian words he explained all the steps and movements in an enormous and varied quantity of ballets.

Petipa liked his dancers to have a Classical perfection and purity of style; but even his great display pieces had to convey emotion and feeling. That he loved pretty women shows in his choreography; just as the men, in order to carry off their roles have, like the master himself, to possess stage presence and dramatic ability, as well as technical ability.

At the end of fifty-six years with the Maryinski Theatre, fashion turned against Petipa. He was told to retire even though Fokine, one of the new innovators, said that his work was not in decline — just the opposite. During Petipa's time the Maryinski had become the most polished company there had ever been.

Embittered by the misfortunes of his last days, Marius Petipa, the 'Father of Classical Ballet', died on 14th July, 1910 at Gurzuf in the Crimea. At the time of his death there was little comment, and the company was on holiday.

Thirty years after *The Sleeping Beauty* was first performed in Russia, Diaghilev brought the ballet to London — and lost a fortune — at the Alhambra Theatre. The ballet was staged by Nicolai Sergueyev (who had been régisseur at the Maryinski Theatre) with sets and costumes by Bakst.

Sergueyev had fled from Communist Russia taking with him the production notes from the Maryinski Theatre. These notes, combined with some extra choreography by Ninette de Valois and Frederick Ashton, formed the basis of the Royal Ballet production.

The Sleeping Beauty ballet opened the Royal Opera House on 20th February, 1946, after the long war years during which time the theatre had been used as a dance hall.

The Sleeping Beauty Prologue, Act 1, Act 4 Backcloth

STAGE DIRECTIONS

N.B.: SLIDE SETS ON TO STAGE MAKING SURE THAT THE EDGES ARE FLUSH WITH SIDES OF THEATRE.

- PROLOGUE: The Christening
Cattalabutte: 16. Baby Aurora's cradle and nurse: 12. King and Queen: 17. Ladies-in-Waiting: 7. Pages: 8. Fairy of the Crystal Fountain, her cavalier and page: 14. Fairy of the Enchanted Garden, her cavalier and page: 15. Fairy of the Woodland Glades, her cavalier and page: 4. Fairy of the Song Birds, her cavalier and page: 18. Fairy of the Golden Vine, her cavalier and page: 10. Lilac Fairy: 13, her cavalier and page: 5, her attendants: 6, 11. Carabosse, coach and rats: 20, 21. Heralds: 9. Courtiers, guards.

- Drop Palace backcloth into grid slot 8. Slide set on to stage. Drop ceiling drapes into grid slot 3.

- Lift Tabs. Drop Tabs after end of Prologue.

- Act 1: The Spell
Cattalabutte: 18. King and Queen: 5. Village girls with garlands: 9, 10, 12, 13. Aurora and English Prince: 22, her friends: 15, 16. Spanish Prince, Indian Prince, French Prince: 21. Carabosse: 3. Youths: 8, 11, 14. Courtiers.

- Leave Palace backcloth in grid slot 8. Slide set on to stage. Lift Tabs. Drop Tabs after end of Act 1.

- Act 4: The Wedding
Cattalabutte: 21. King and Queen: 22. Prince Florestan and his sisters: 18. Bluebird and Princess Florine: 20. Red Riding Hood and the Wolf: 17. Beauty and the Beast: 19. Hop-o'-my-Thumb: 16. Princess Aurora and Prince Florimund: 24. Three Ivans: 14. Polish dancers: 7, 8, 11, 12, 13. Lilac Fairy: 4 and her attendants: 3, 5. Heralds: 1, 2.

- Drop Palace backcloth into grid slot 8. Slide set on to stage. Drop ceiling drapes into grid slot 4.

- Lift Tabs. Drop Tabs after end of Act 4.

THE SLEEPING BEAUTY Prologue: The Christening

Cut out the pieces along the black lines, score and fold as shown on p. 5.

Keep the pieces carefully.

Before glueing, make sure that the folded pieces match the shapes of the finished model on the photograph.

Matching glue tracks have either matching capital letters, numbers or small numbered letters.

Make sure the pieces are in the correct position before glueing.

Glue the pieces in the following order:
- Cut out Palace backcloth and glue to hanger along glue track.

STAGE RIGHT COLONNADE
- Glue rostrums A and A1 to stage floor where indicated.
- Fold colonnade and glue starting from a1 on front of rostrum to a13 back of scenery. Centre section a4 to be found on p. 65.

CENTRE COLONNADE
- Glue rostrum B to stage floor where indicated.
- Glue front colonnade to rostrum b1, b2.
- Glue back colonnade to rostrum b3, b4, and to rear of front colonnade b5, b6.

ENTRANCE GATE
- Glue gate to stage floor, C1, C2, C3, C4.
- Glue side of gateway to end colonnade C5.

DAIS
- Glue rostrum D to stage floor where indicated.
- Glue column and dais draperies to rostrum d3, d4, d5.
- Glue battens d6 between back colonnade and dais.

FLATS
- Glue braces 1 and 2 to flats 1 and 2.
- Glue braces 1 and 2 to stage floor spaces marked 1 and 2.

DANCERS
- Fold back flaps, glue along lines on the stage floor, on top of the small matching numbers.

CEILING DRAPERIES
- Glue to hanger along glue track.

▲ STAGE RIGHT

STAGE LEFT ▼

DO NOT CUT OUT from this side

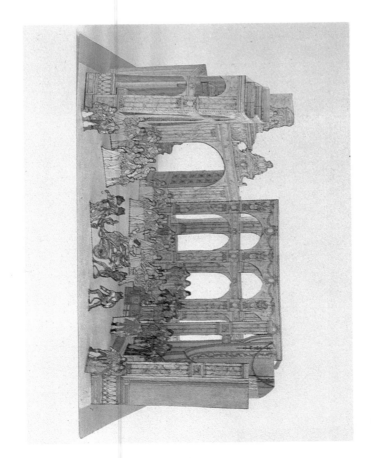

87

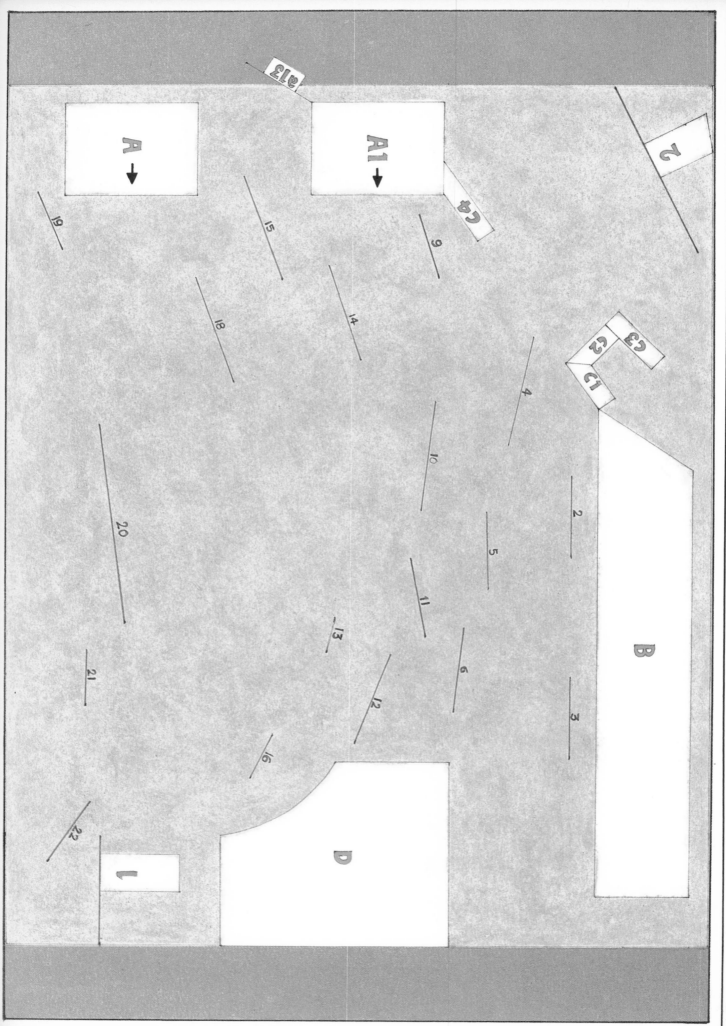

The Sleeping Beauty Prologue Stage floor   CUT OUT from this side

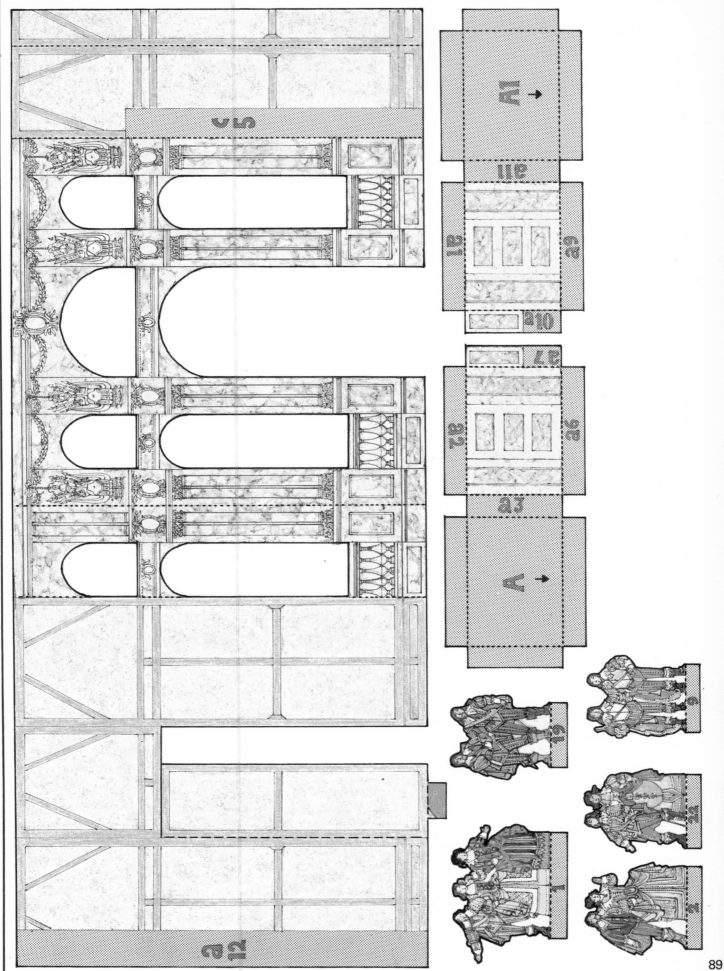

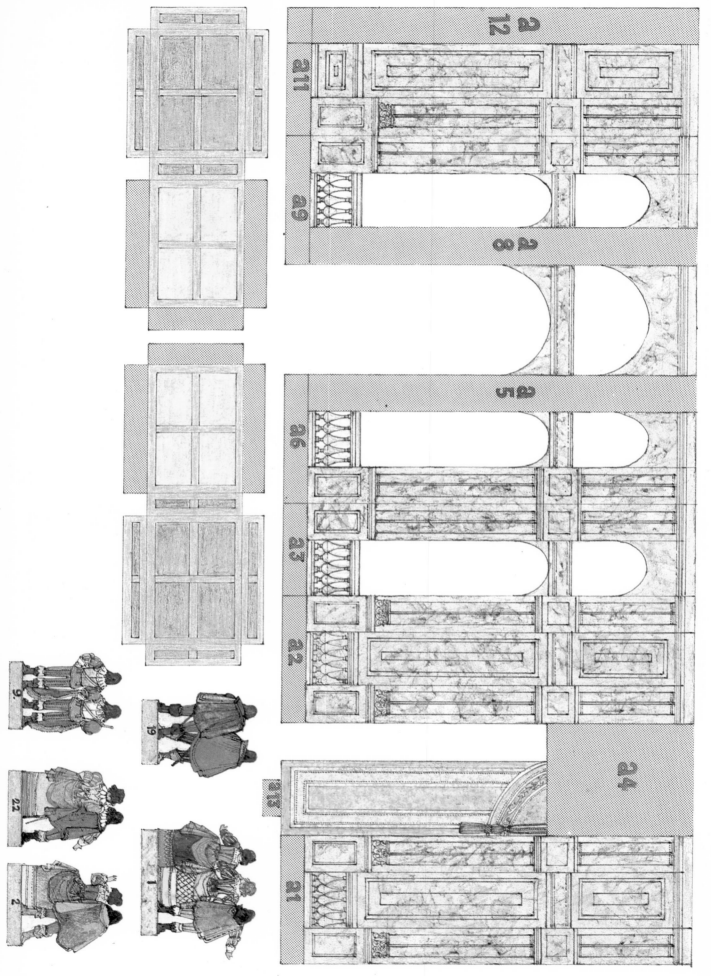

✂ CUT OUT from this side   **Prologue** Stage centre: rostrum and front colonnade; entrance gate; fountain flat

Labels on parts: b3, b4, b1, B, b2, b5, b6, b7, b8, b9, 19, 20, 21

91

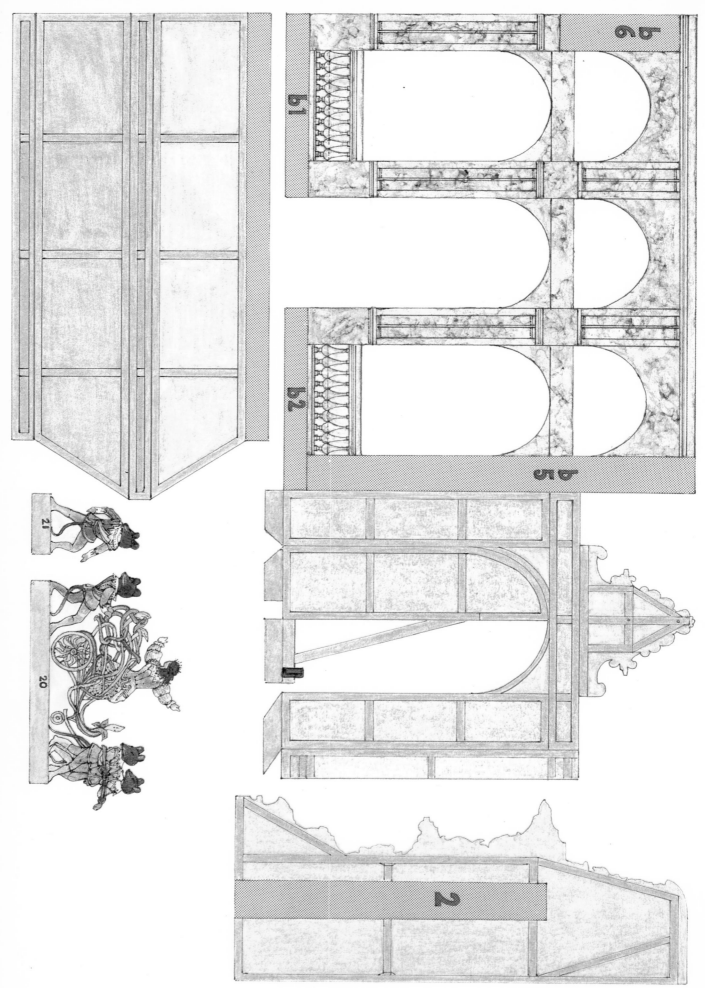

b1

b2

20

21

2

Prologue Stage centre: back colonnade; flat; brace

9

p

b3

b4

b3

11

9

13

5

10

4

18

15

14

93

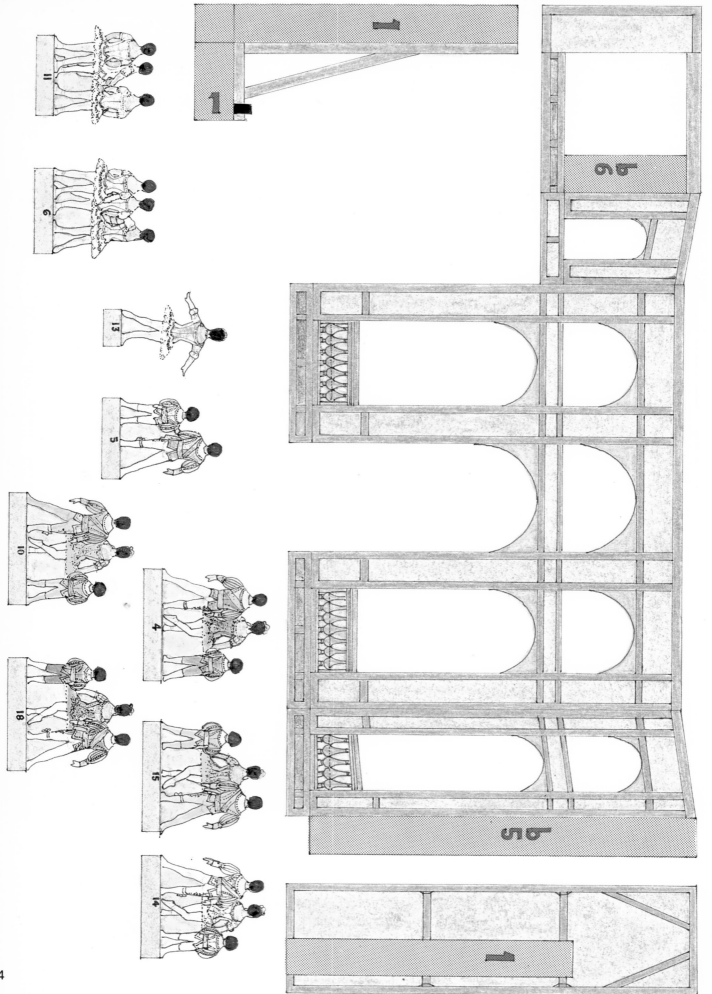

94

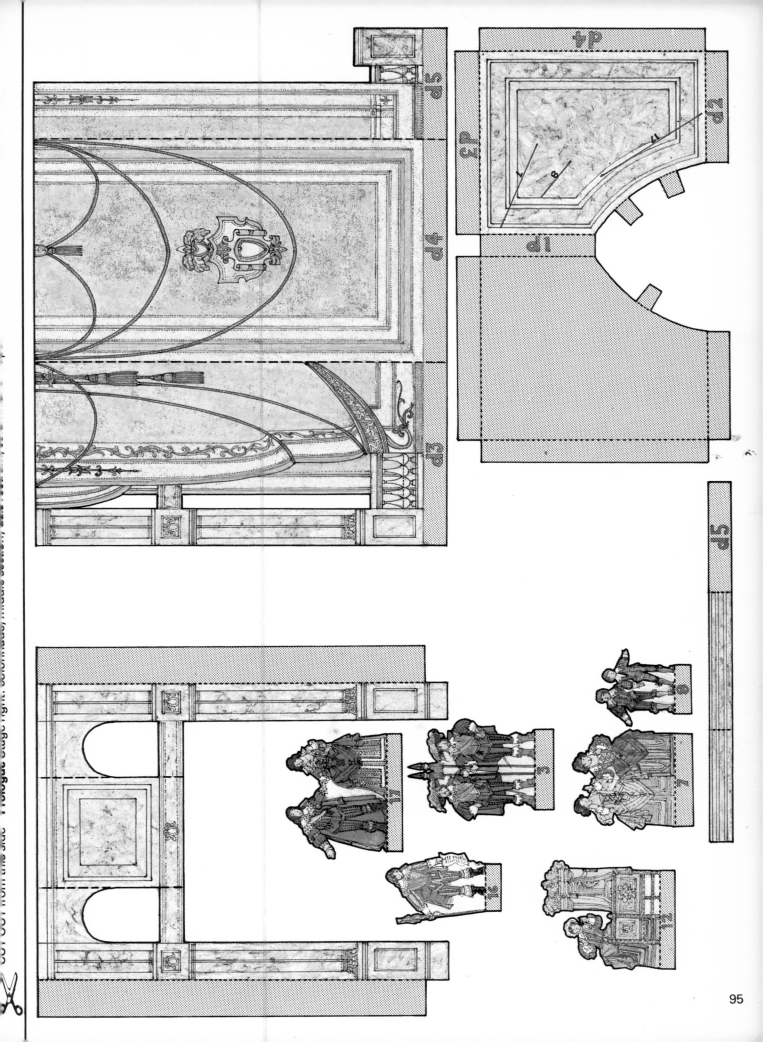

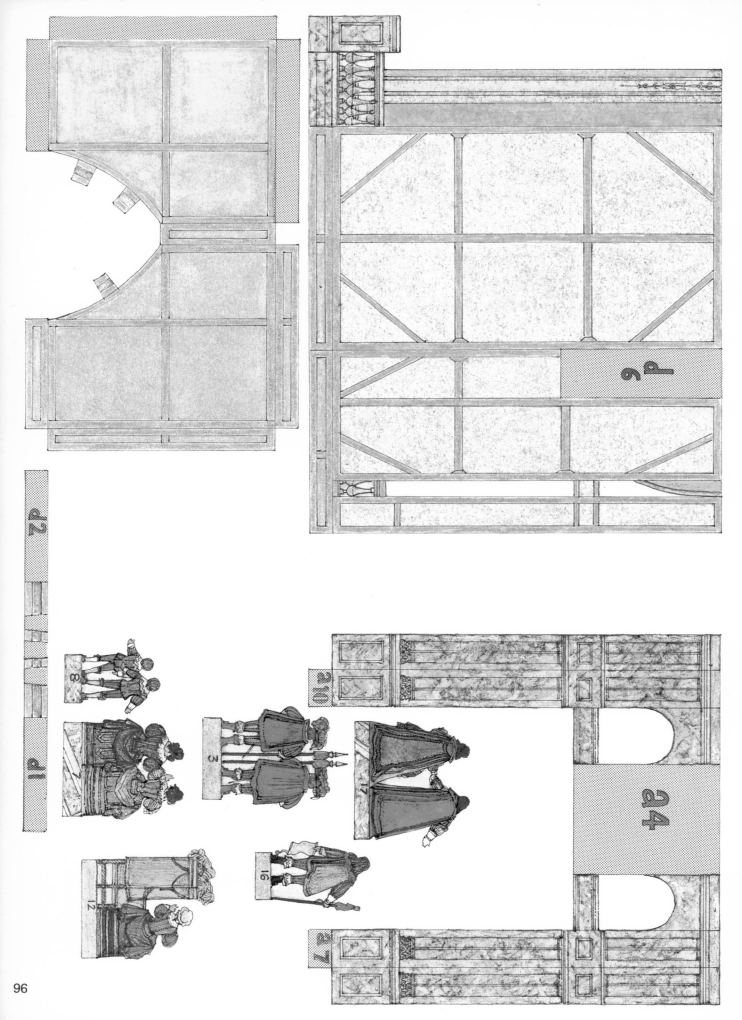

96

CUT OUT from this side · **Prologue** ceiling draperies, brace, hanger for Palace backcloth

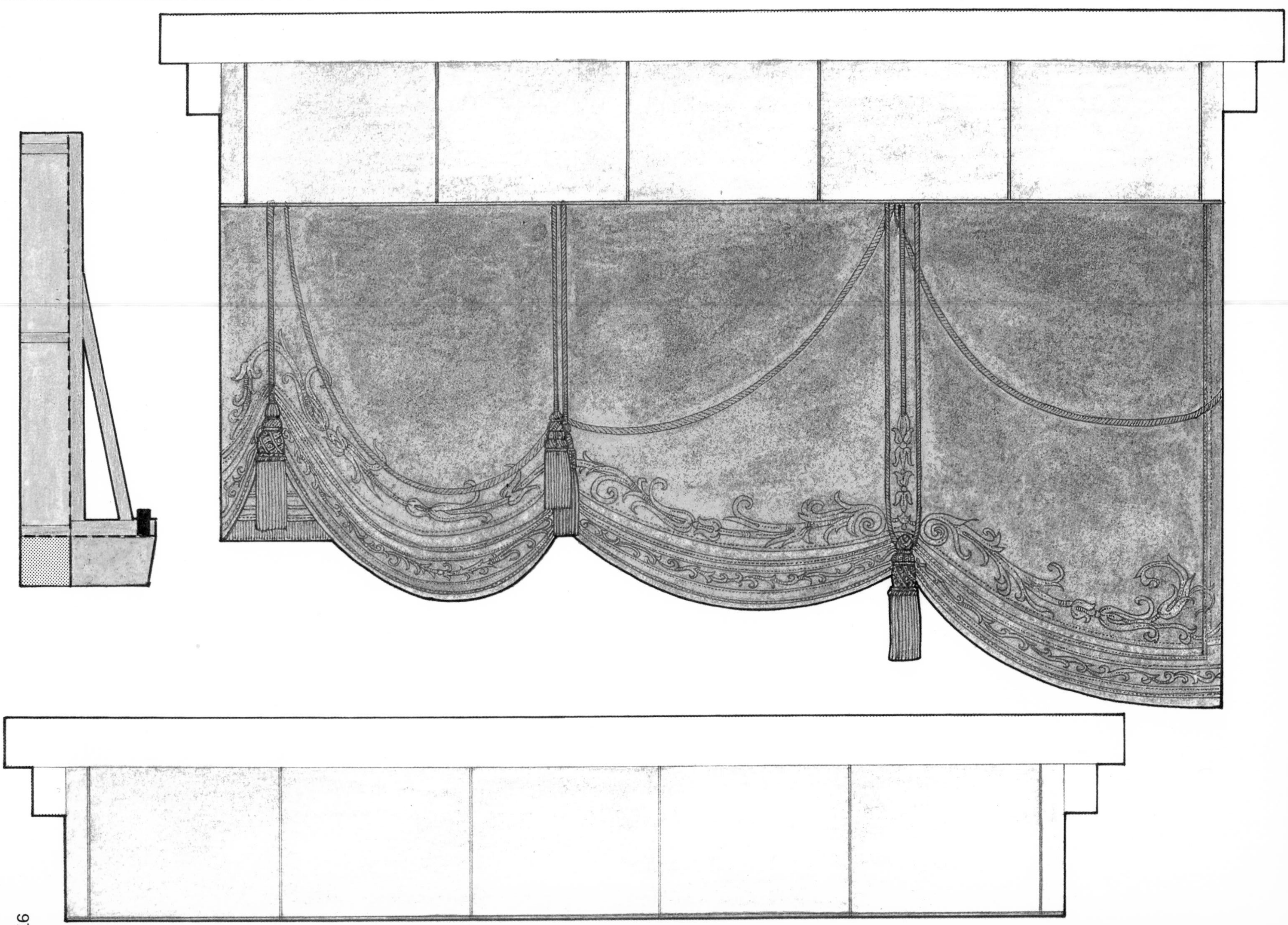

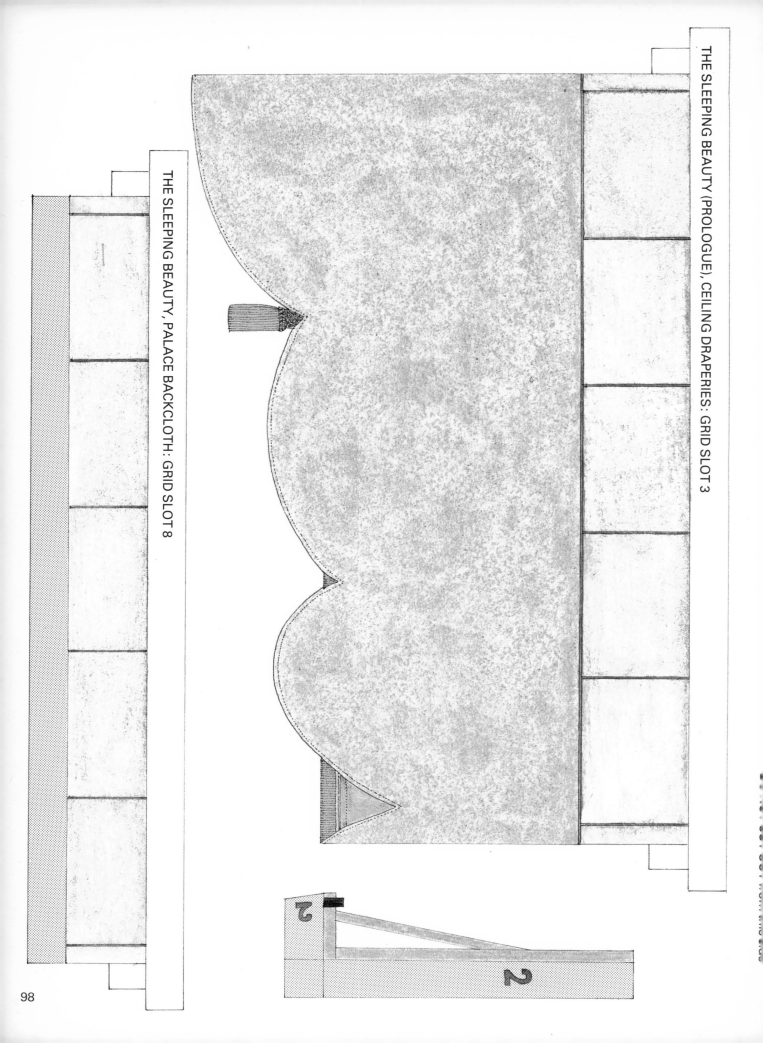

THE SLEEPING BEAUTY (PROLOGUE), CEILING DRAPERIES: GRID SLOT 3

THE SLEEPING BEAUTY, PALACE BACKCLOTH: GRID SLOT 8

2

2

THE SLEEPING BEAUTY   Act 1: The Spell

Cut out the pieces along the black lines, score and fold as shown on p. 5.

Keep pieces marked A, B, C and dancers in separate groups.

Before glueing, make sure that the folded pieces match the shapes of the finished model on the photograph.

Matching glue tracks have either matching capital letters or numbered letters.

Make sure the pieces are in the correct position before glueing.

Glue the pieces in the following order:

STAGE RIGHT TRELLIS
- Glue rostrum A to stage floor where indicated.
- Glue trellis section A1, A2 to rostrum. Glue A3. Slot together, fold flaps back and glue roof A4, A5.
- Glue trellis section A6, A7 to rostrum. Glue A8. Slot together, fold flaps back and glue roof A9, A10.
- Glue the steps band to front of rostrum A11, A12.
- Glue centre arched roof to both sections of trellis A13, A14, A15.
- Glue centre archway to back of trellis A16, A17, A18.

STAGE CENTRE TRELLIS
- Glue rostrum B to stage floor where indicated.
- Glue centre section B1, B2, B3, B4, B5, B6, B7.
- Glue centre arched roof B8, B9, B10.
- Glue trellis section B11, B12, B13, B14.
- Glue trellis section B15, B16, B17, B18.
- Glue the steps band to front of rostrum B19, B20.
- Glue statues B21, B22 to stage floor where indicated.
- Glue trellis behind statues to back of trellis sections B23, B24, B25, B26.
- Slot together, fold flaps back and glue roof B27, B28 and roof B29, B30.

STAGE LEFT TRELLIS
- Glue rostrum C to stage floor where indicated.
- Glue trellis section C1, C2 to rostrum, C3 to side, C4 to floor.
- Slot together, fold flaps back and glue roof C5, C6.
- Glue trellis section C7, C8 to rostrum, C9 to side, C10 to floor.
- Slot together, fold flaps back and glue roof C11, C12.
- Glue the steps band to front of rostrum C13, C14.

CUPOLA FOR STAGE LEFT TRELLIS
- Glue section of cupola C15, C16 to front piece.
- Glue cupola front piece C17, C18 to both trellis sections.
- Glue section of cupola C19, C20 to both trellis sections.
- Glue back section of cupola C19, C20 to both trellis sections.

CENTRE SECTION OF STAGE LEFT TRELLIS
- Glue trellis to both sections C23, C24. Glue C25 to back of cupola, C26 to rostrum.

DANCERS AND TREES
- Fold back flaps, glue along lines on the stage floor on top of the small matching numbers.

ARCHWAYS
- Link stage right trellis to centre trellis and stage left trellis to centre trellis by glueing hedge archways D1, D3 and E1, E3; then back trellis D2, D4 and E2, E4.

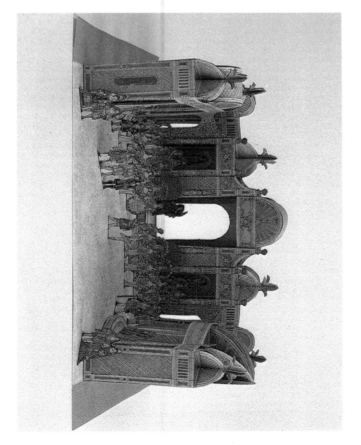

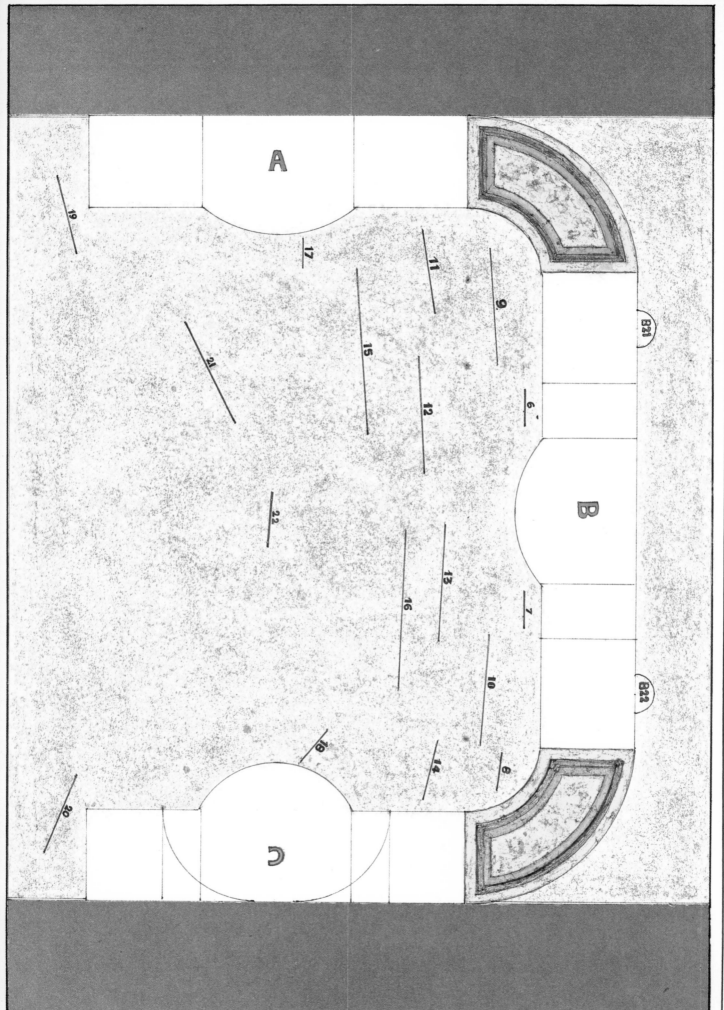

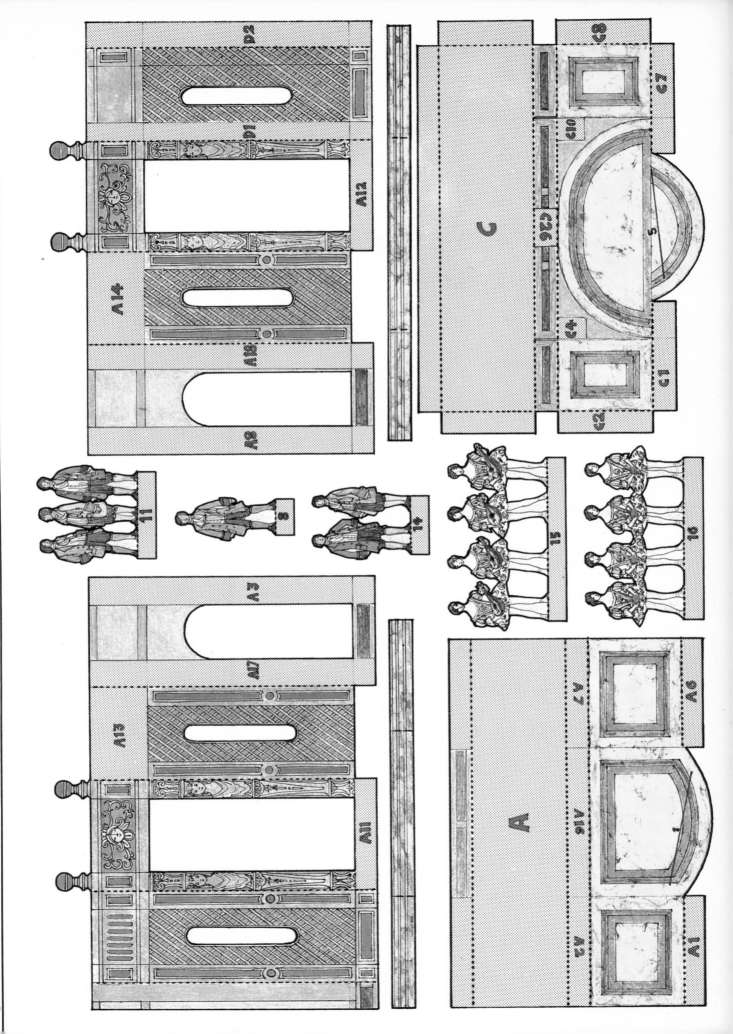

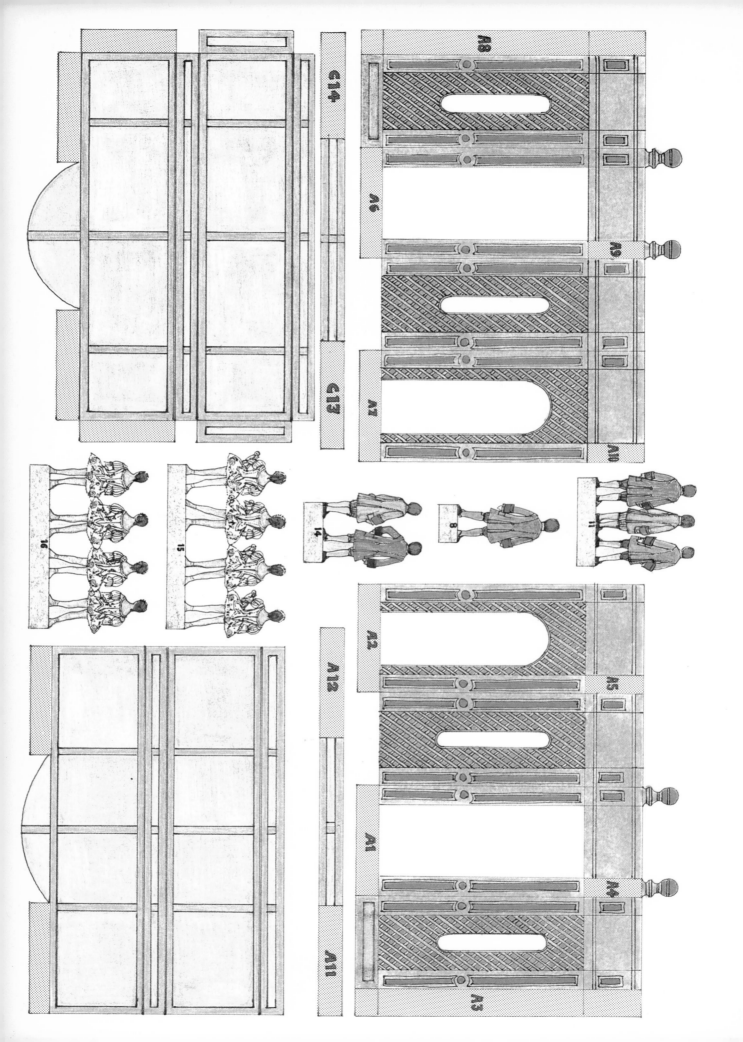

C14

C13

A8

A6

A9

A7

A10

16

15

14

8

11

A2

A5

A12

A1

A4

A11

A3

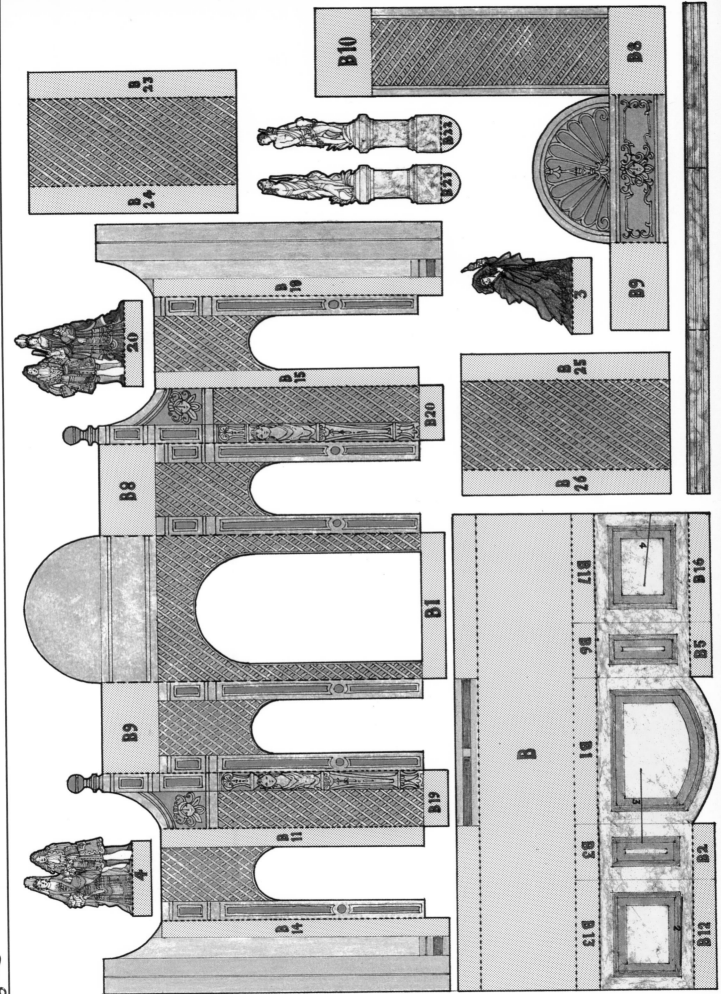

B 20

B 19

B 10

E 2

B 16

3

B 6

B 7

B 5

B 4

B 3

B 2

D 4

20

4

DO NOT CUT OUT from this side

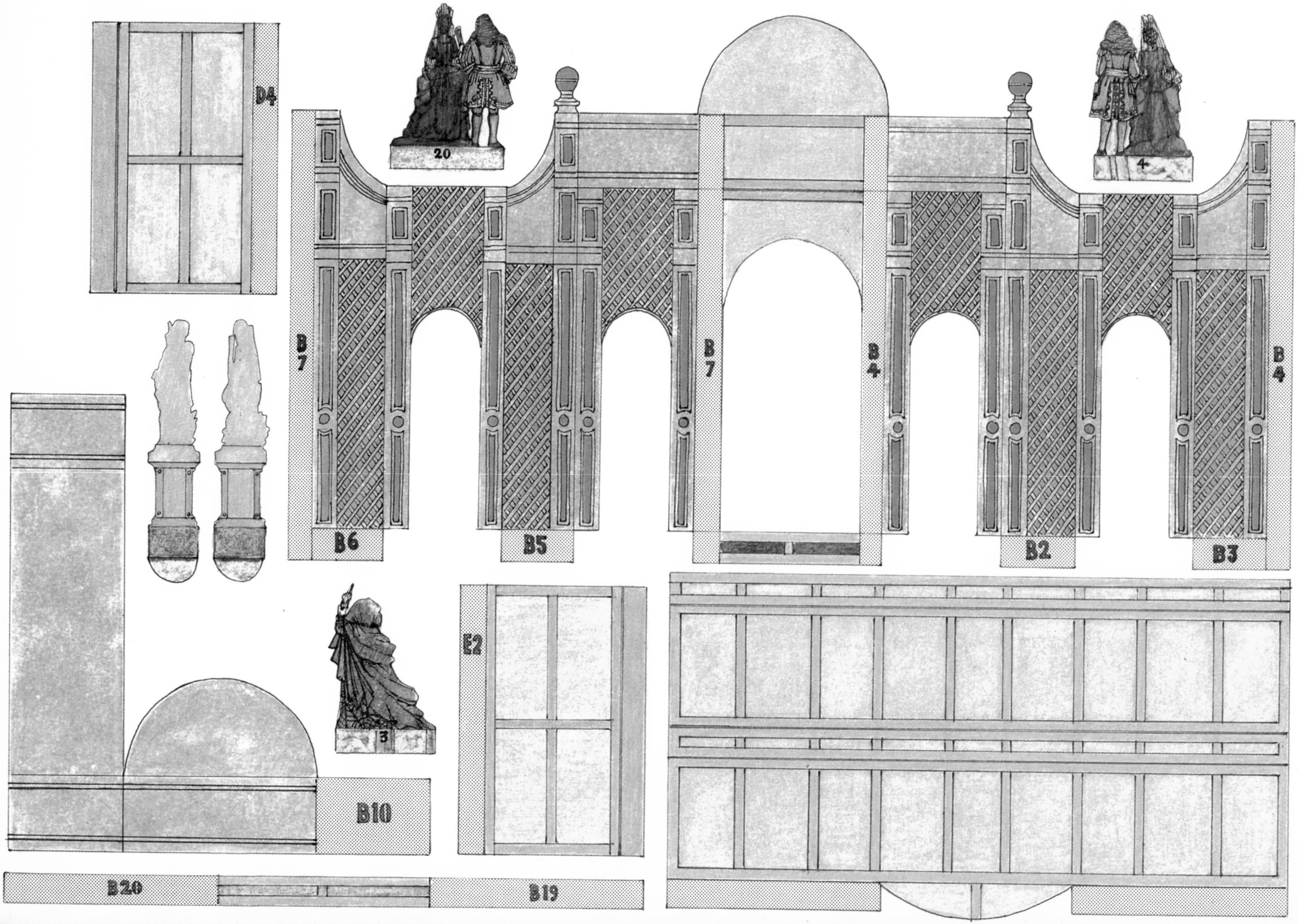

E5

E11

B
26

B
25

E
1

B20

B
15

B
11

B19

D
3

B
24

B
23

D5

E3

E11

E2

D4

D2

B
11

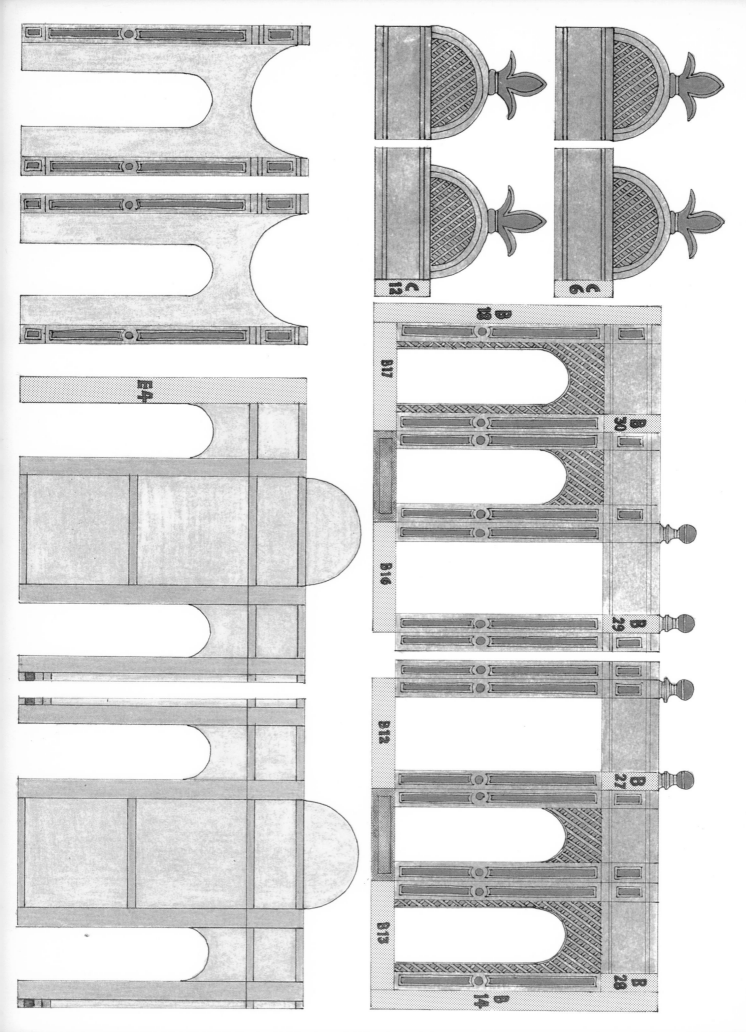

A15

A14

A18

A16

A17

A13

A11

4

2

C21

C17

C9

C23

C14

20

19

18

C22

C18

C3

E5

24

C13

E4

1

C25

C23

C26

C24

9

13

12

10

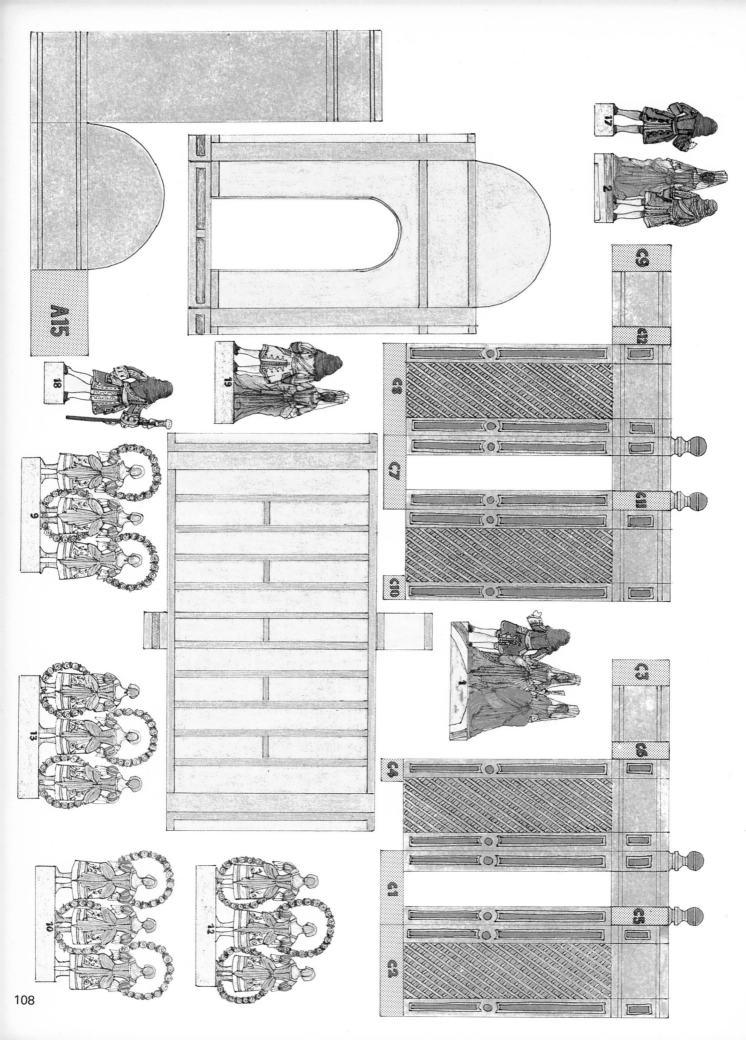

A15

C9

C12

C8

C7

C11

C10

18

19

9

13

10

12

17

2

1

C3

C6

C4

C1

C5

C2

M

29

B
27

D 26

5

21

22

C21

C19

C17

C22

C20

C18

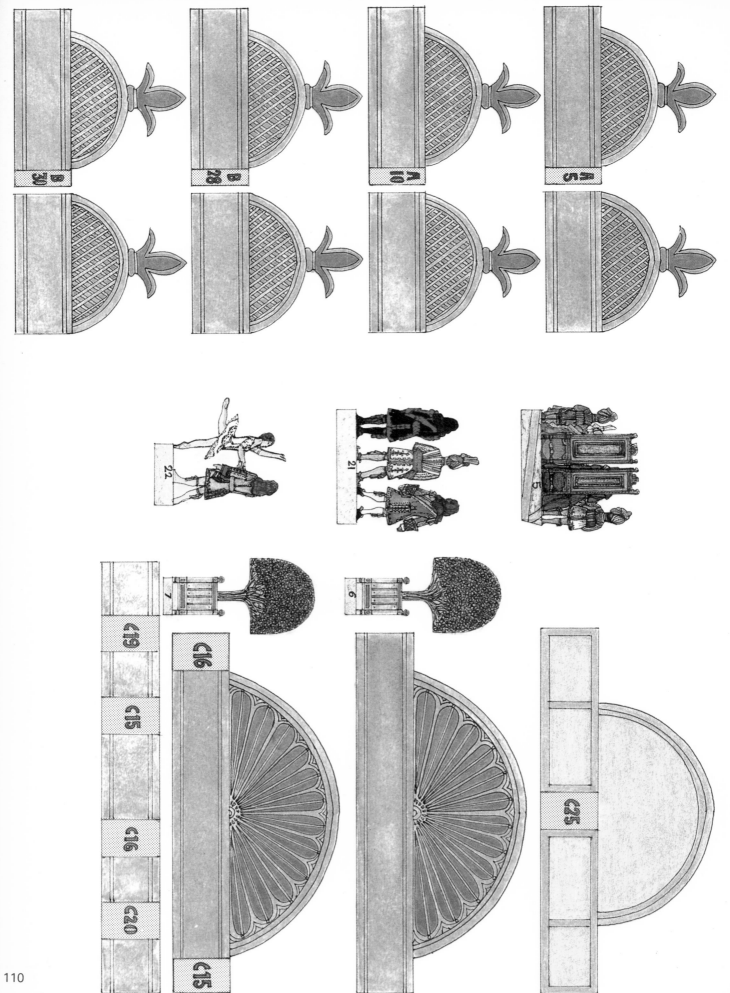

110

DO NOT CUT OUT from this side

STAGE DIRECTIONS

N.B.: SLIDE SETS ON TO STAGE, MAKING SURE THAT THE EDGES ARE FLUSH WITH SIDES OF THEATRE.

• ACT 2: The Vision
  SCENE 1
  Prince Florimund, the Countess, Courtiers 1. Gallison, Courtiers 2. Courtiers 3. Courtiers 2. Hunt attendants and Village girls 4, 5.
  ● Drop this backcloth into grid slot 7.
  ● Drop lakeside trees cut cloth into grid slot 6.
  ● Place tree flats 1, 2 stage right; place tree flats 3, 4 stage left to line up with stage floor, square centre section. Do not glue.
  ● Place dancers centre stage. Do not glue.
  ● Lift tabs.
  SCENE 2
  Lilac Fairy, Prince Florimund 6.
  ● Remove dancers.
  ● Gradually slide in Lilac Fairy's boat on its lake floor between this lake backcloth and the lakeside trees cut cloth from stage left, pull out slowly to stage right.
  NO TABS, RUN THROUGH FOR:

• ACT 3: The Awakening
  Lilac Fairy, Prince Florimund 1. Carabosse and attendants 2. Princess Aurora 7. Nurse 9. Courtiers, Guards.
  ● Leave this backcloth in place.
  ● Drop Palace gate cut cloth into grid slot 2.
  ● Remove Lilac Fairy's boat and trees flats 1, 2, 3, 4.
  ● Slide 'Awakening' set from stage left. Lilac Fairy, Prince Florimund and Carabosse will automatically be in front of Palace gate cut cloth.
  ● Drop decorated ceiling and drapes of Princess Aurora's bedchamber into grid slot 5.
  ● Lift Palace gate cut cloth.
  ● Drop Tabs after end of Act 3.

111

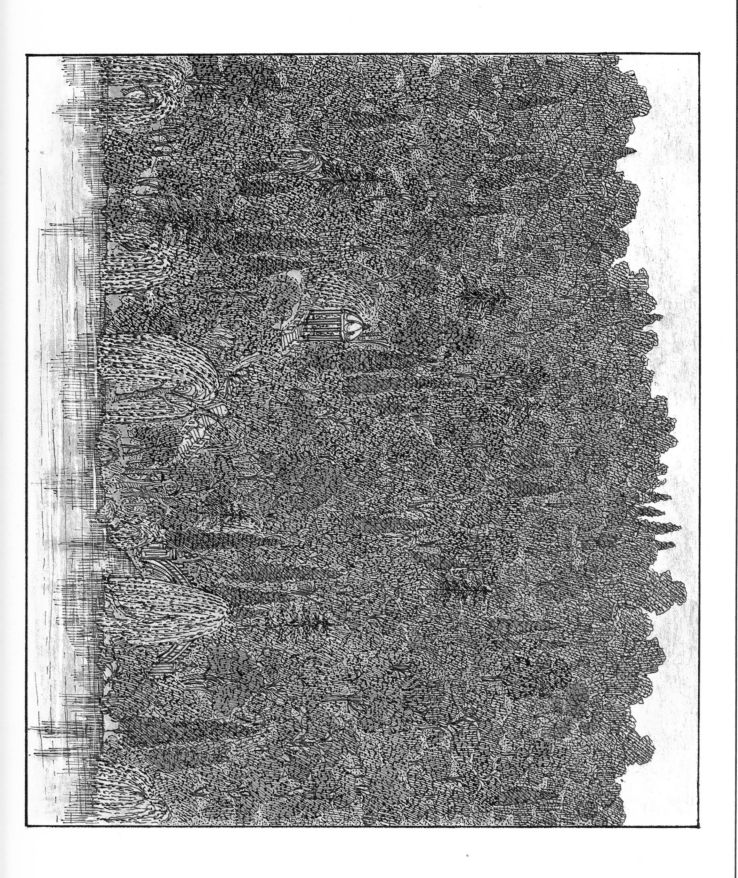

Lake backcloth   CUT OUT from this side

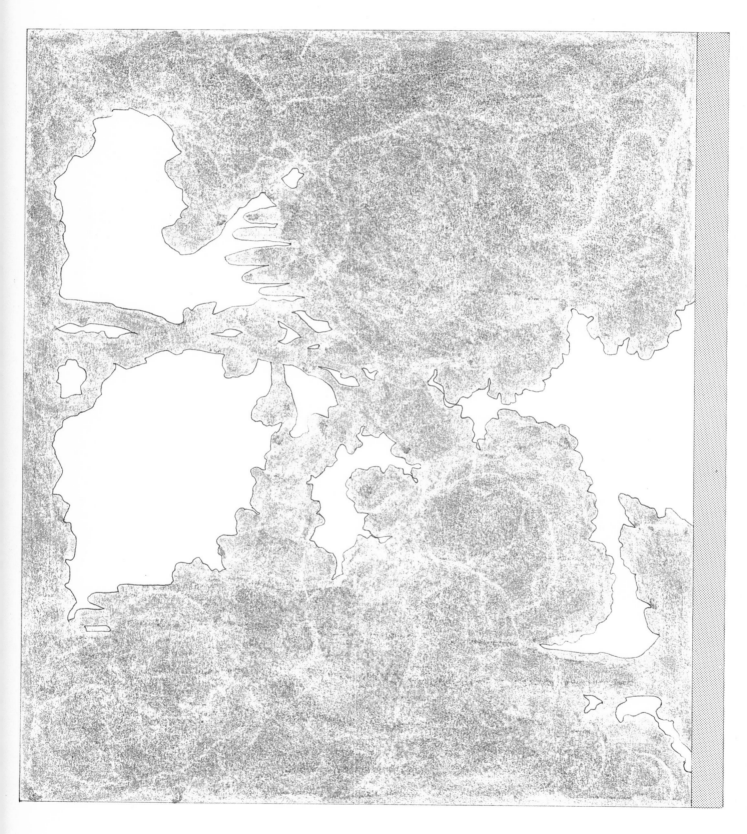

114

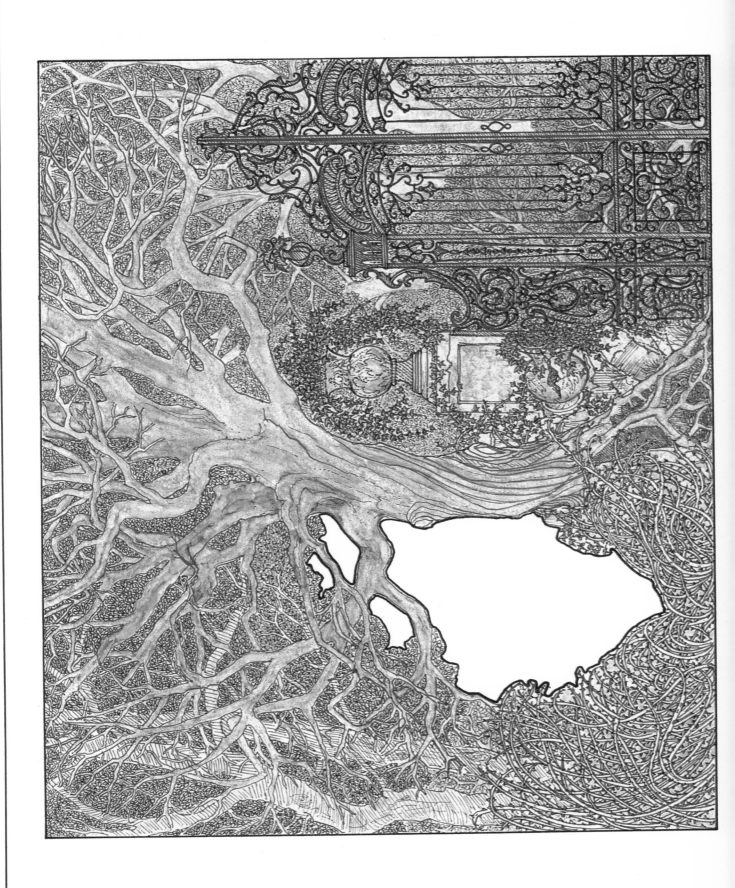

116

Act 2 Stage floor, scene 1; lake floor, scene 2; 3 hangers for backcloths and cut cloths

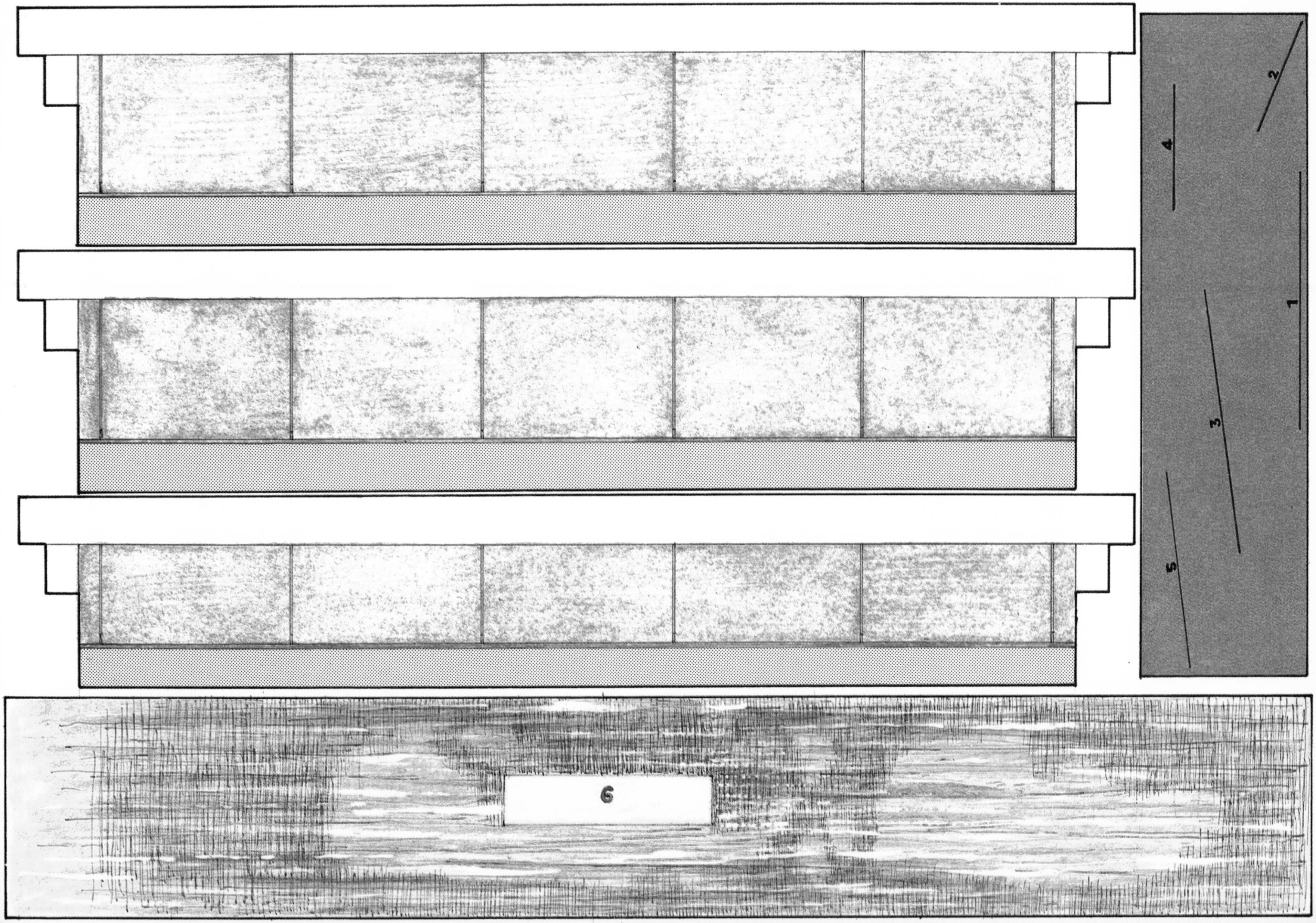

1

2

3

4

5

6

THE SLEEPING BEAUTY Act 2: The Vision, Scene 1.
DANCERS

Fold back flaps, glue along lines on top of matching small numbers.
Prince Florimund, the Countess, Courtiers: 1. Courtiers: 2. Gallison and Courtiers: 3. Hunt attendants and Village girls: 4, 5.

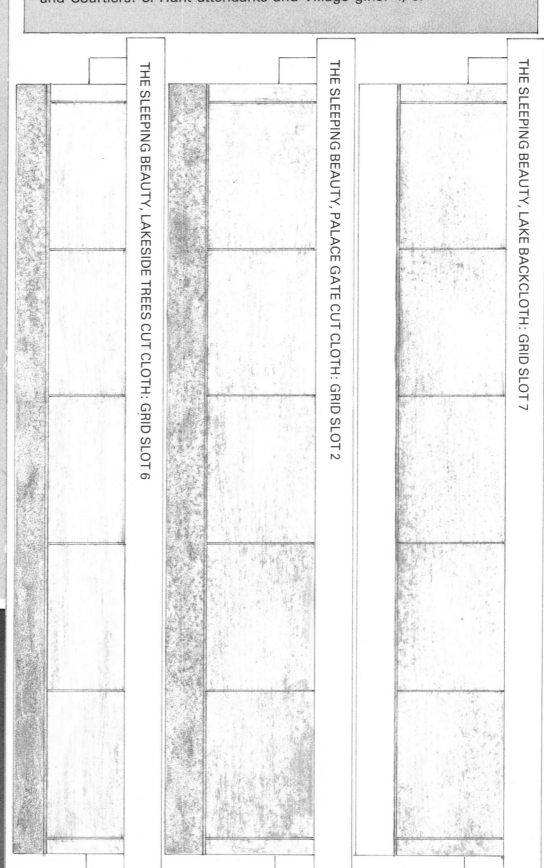

THE SLEEPING BEAUTY, LAKESIDE TREES CUT CLOTH: GRID SLOT 6

THE SLEEPING BEAUTY, PALACE GATE CUT CLOTH: GRID SLOT 2

THE SLEEPING BEAUTY, LAKE BACKCLOTH: GRID SLOT 7

DO NOT CUT OUT from this side

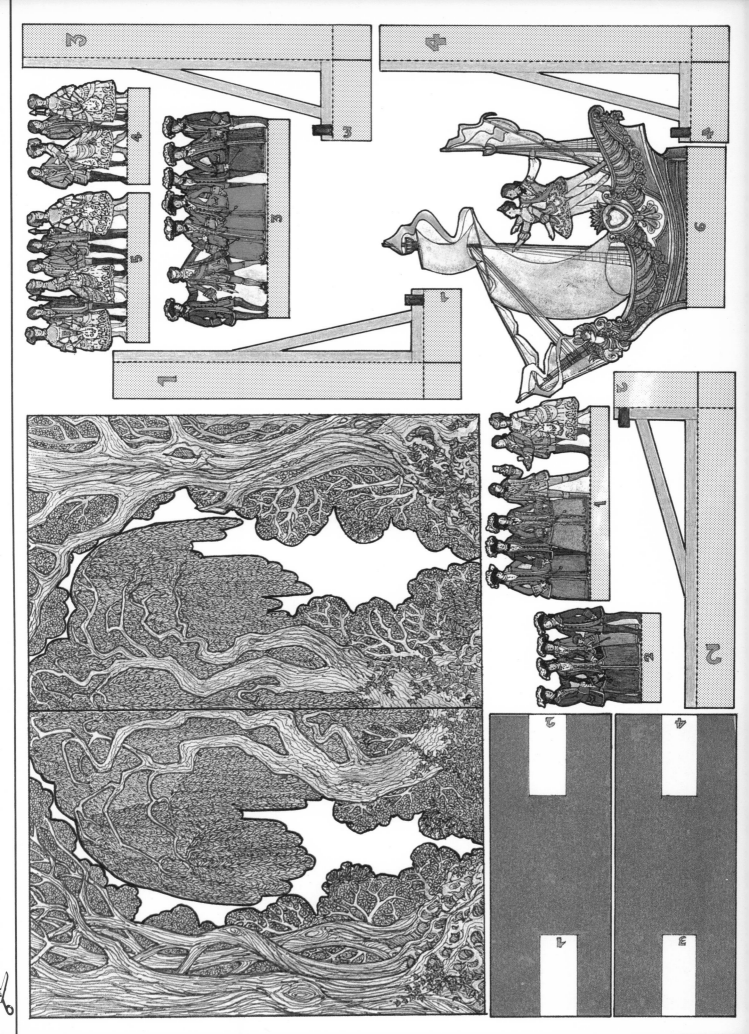

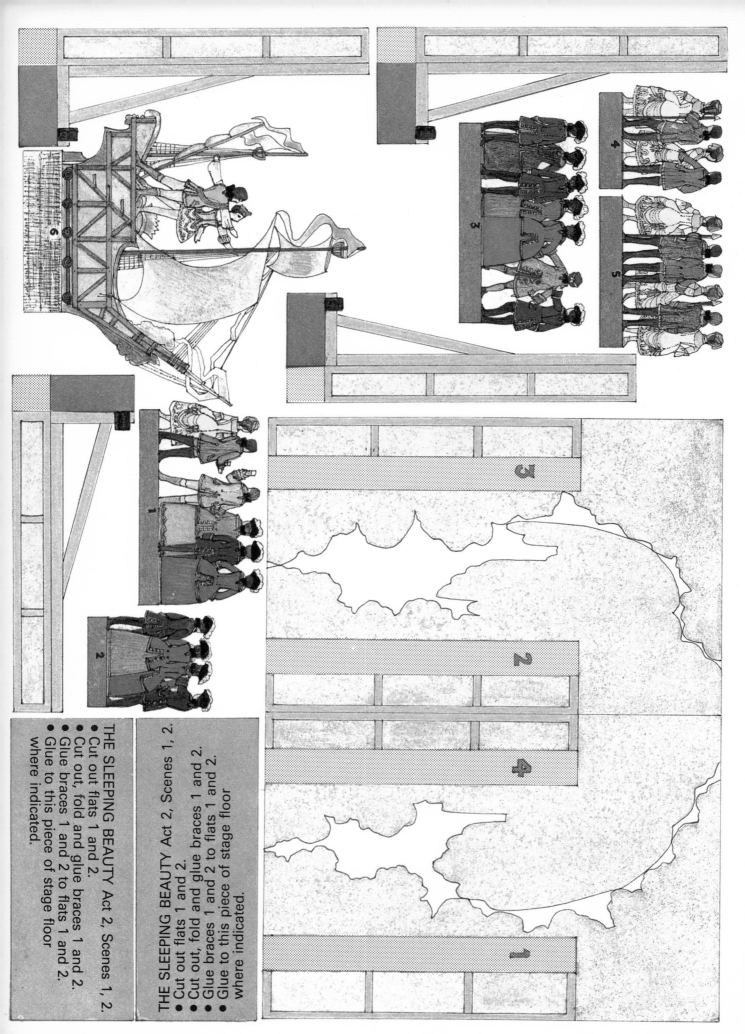

THE SLEEPING BEAUTY Act 2, Scenes 1, 2.

THE SLEEPING BEAUTY Act 2, Scenes 1, 2.
● Cut out flats 1 and 2.
● Cut out, fold and glue braces 1 and 2.
● Glue braces 1 and 2 to flats 1 and 2.
● Glue to this piece of stage floor where indicated.

THE SLEEPING BEAUTY Act 3: The Awakening

Cut out the pieces along the black lines, score and fold as shown on p. 5.
Keep the pieces carefully.
Before glueing make sure that the folded pieces match the shapes of the finished model on the photograph.
Matching glue tracks have matching capital letters, numbers and small letters.
Make sure the pieces are in the correct position before glueing.

Cut out and fold open doors and windows of bedchamber wall A, B, C.
Glue the pieces in the following order:

- Glue rostrum A, B, C and all its glue track to stage floor where indicated.
- Glue the steps band r, s to front of rostrum.
- Glue bedchamber wall a, b, c to back of rostrum.
- Glue anteroom rostrum D to back of bedchamber wall a1 and to stage floor where indicated.
- Glue anteroom rostrum E to back of bedchamber wall e1 and to stage floor where indicated.
- Glue flat d to rostrum D.
- Glue flat e to rostrum E.
- Glue balustrade t to rostrum floor.
- Glue curtain 9 to balustrade, fold back and glue to track at the back of bedchamber wall a.
- Glue bed q to bed head q.
- Glue drapes h, g, i to pelmet h, g, i.
- Glue canopy's three pieces together along glue track.
- Glue top feathers.
- Glue finished canopy m, n, o to pelmet m, n, o glue track.
- Glue pelmet flaps k, l to back of bed head k, l.
- Glue back reinforcing panel p to back of bed head p.
- Glue bed 10 to rostrum floor.
- Glue brace 8 to back of bed panel 8, and to stage floor.

DANCERS
- Glue back flaps, glue along lines on the rostrum and stage floors on top of the small matching numbers.

FLATS
- Glue braces 1, 2, 3, 4, 5, 7 to flats 1, 2, 3, 4, 5, 7.
- Glue braces to stage floor where indicated.
- Glue back of flat 6 to rostrum front where indicated.
- Fold flap and glue terrace back flat F to this side of the page (under stage floor) where indicated.

CEILING DRAPERIES
- Glue to hanger along glue track.

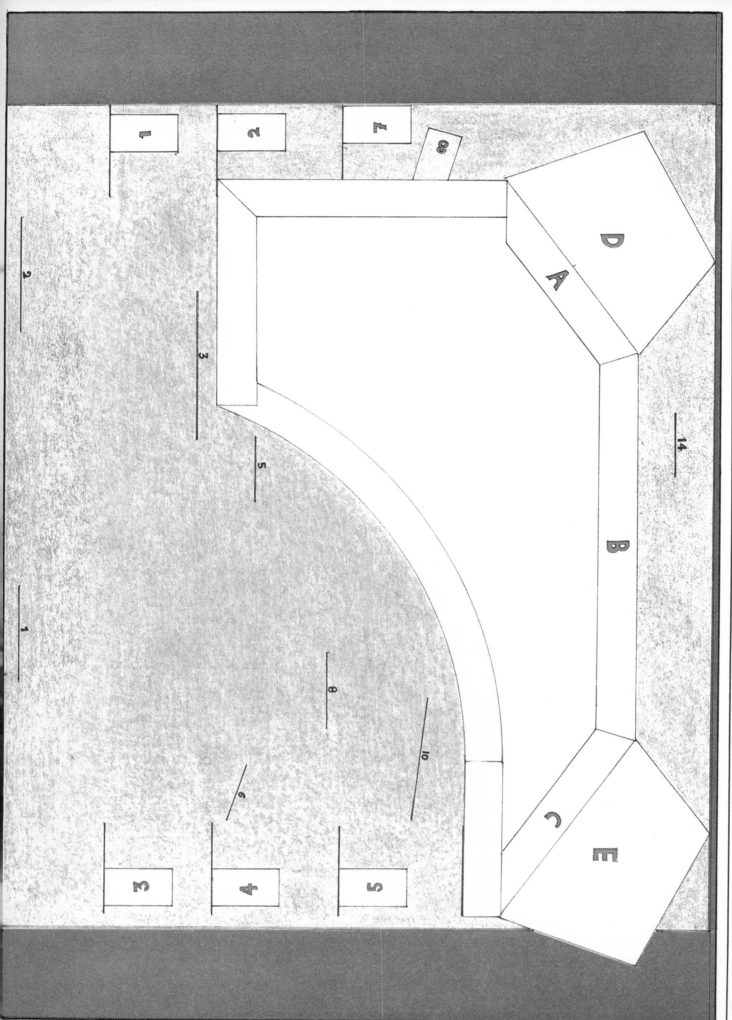

The Sleeping Beauty Act 3 Stage floor   CUT OUT from this side

1
2
3
5
6.
9.
1a
1b
2a
2
3a
3
4
4
5
6
6
7a
7b
8
9
10
11
12
13
14

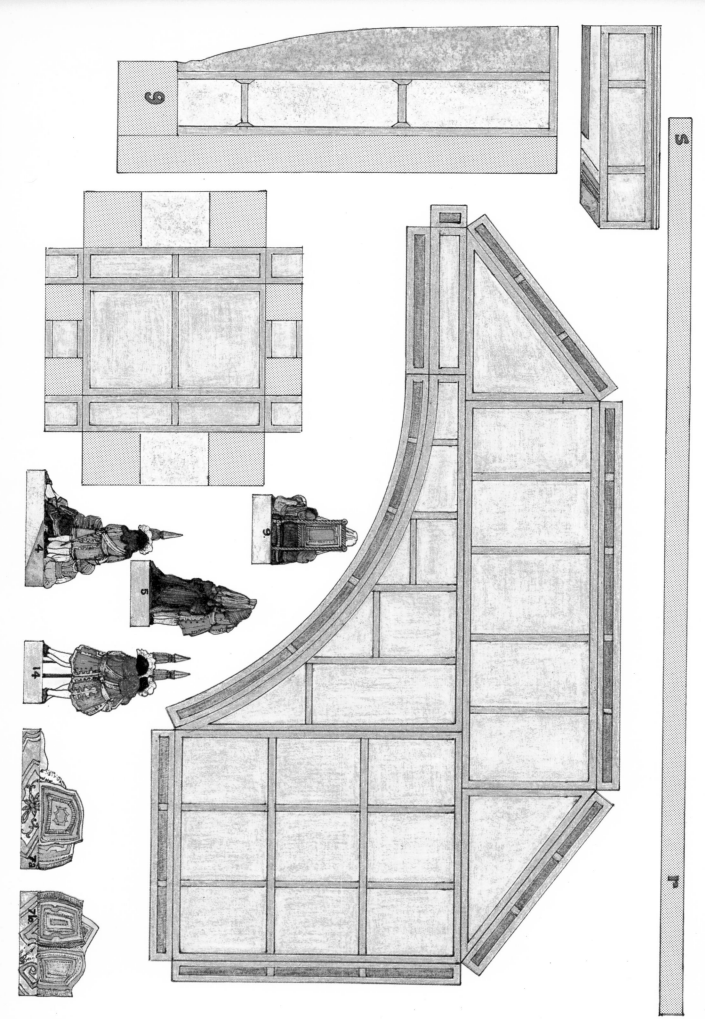

9

s

124

DO NOT CUT OUT from this side

CUT OUT from this side **A.3** Bedchamber walls, bed canopy, drapes and pelmet, flat

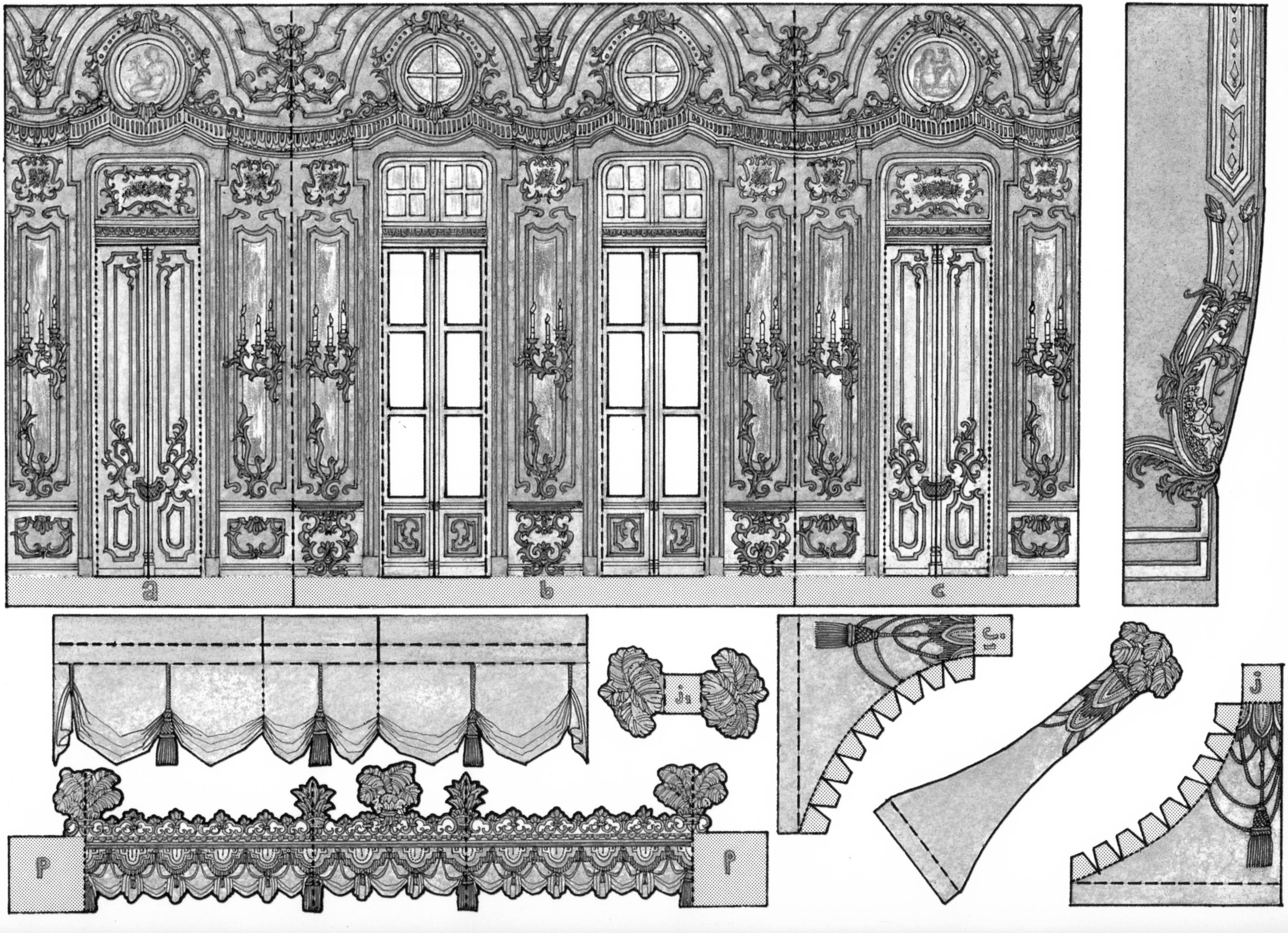

DO NOT CUT OUT from this side

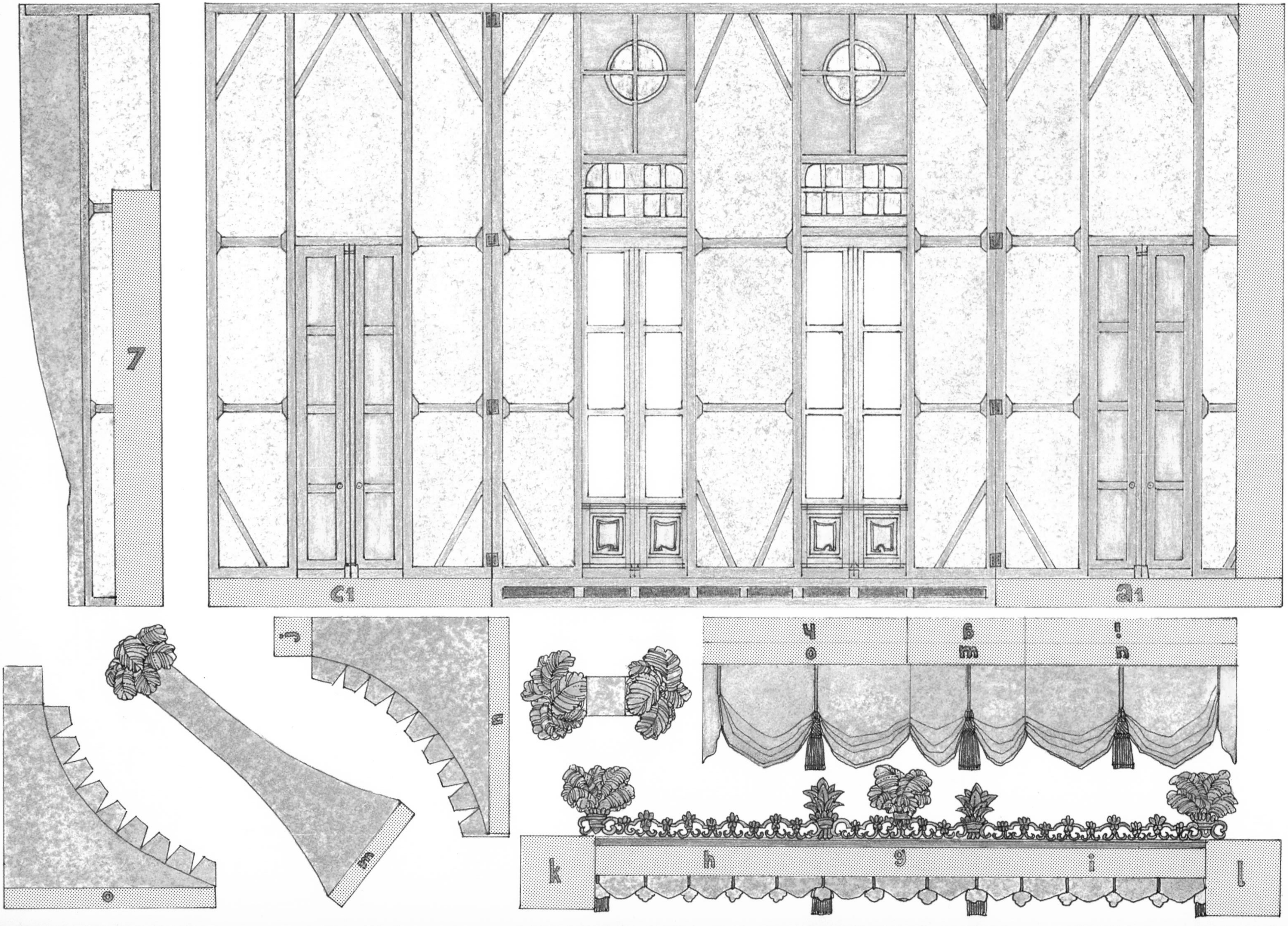

CUT OUT from this side **Act 3** Anterooms: rostrums, flats, bed head and reinforcing panel, braces, back of terrace: flat

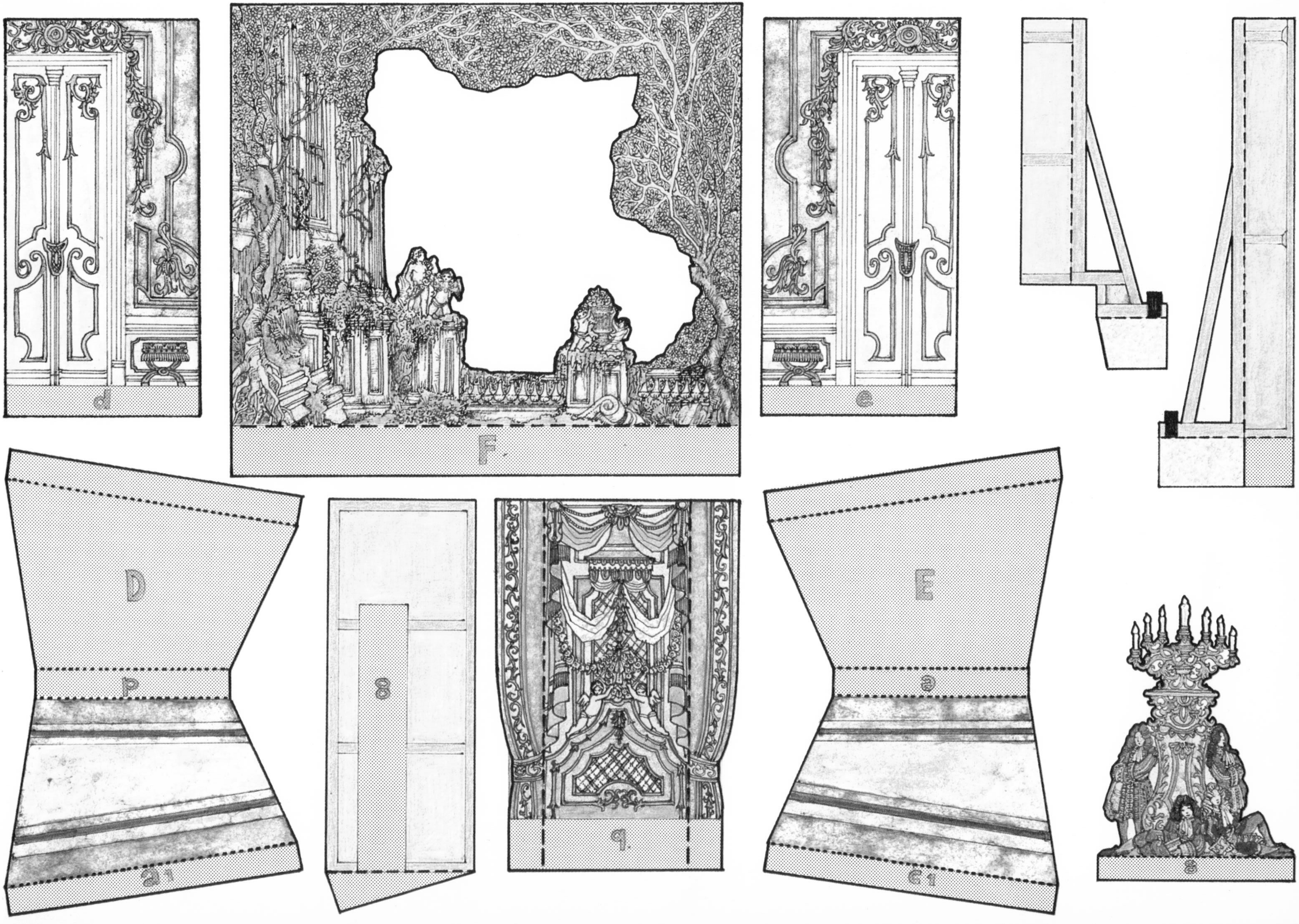

DO NOT CUT OUT from this side

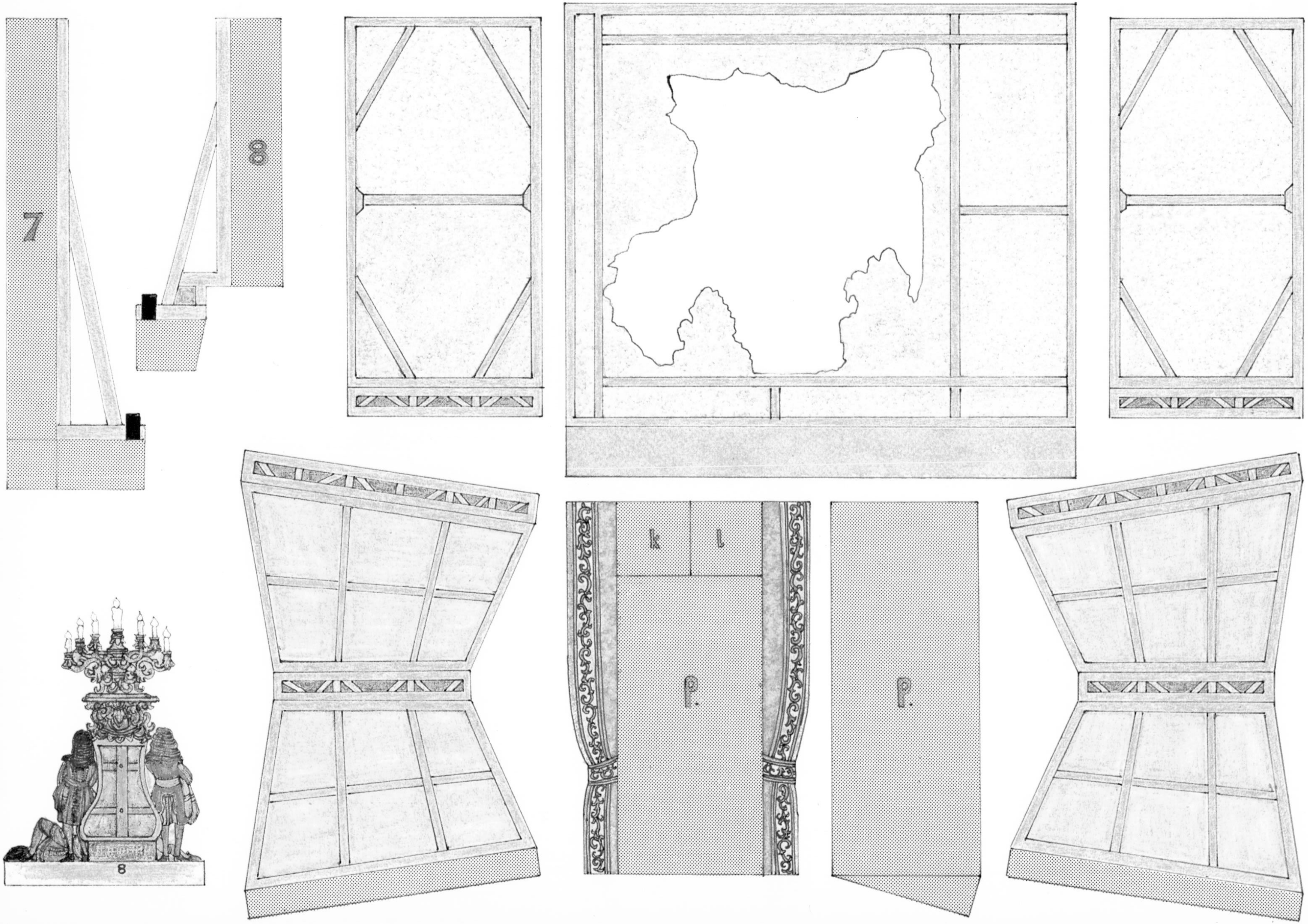

1

2

5

4

3

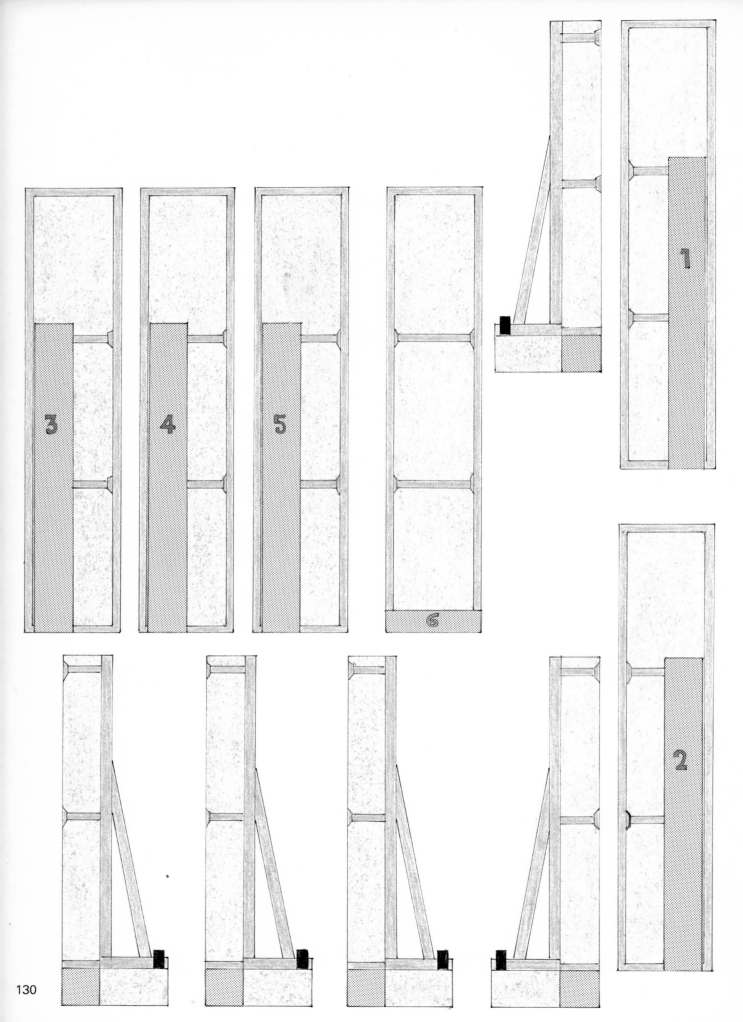

CUT OUT from this side **Act 3** Princess Aurora's bedchamber: ceiling and draperies

DO NOT CUT OUT from this side

THE SLEEPING BEAUTY Act 4: The Wedding

Cut out the pieces along the black lines, score and fold as shown on p. 5.
Keep pieces marked A, B, C, D and dancers in separate groups.
Before glueing, make sure that the folded pieces match the shapes of the finished model on the photograph.
Matching glue tracks have numbered letters.
Make sure the pieces are in the correct position before glueing.

Glue the pieces in the following order:

STAGE CENTRE SECTION

- Glue rostrum A to stage floor where indicated.
- Glue steps band to front of rostrum A1, A2, A3, A4.
- Glue back of decorated columns to rostrum A5, A6, A7, A8.
- Glue other side of decorated columns to previous columns A9, A10; leaving glue tracks B1 and C1 free.
- Glue back wall to stage floor A11, to back of rostrum A12, A13, A14, A15, A16, A17, to stage floor A18.
- Glue centre pelmet to wall A19, to stage right decorated columns A20, A21, to centre of wall A22, A23, to stage left decorated columns A24, A25, to wall A26.

STAGE RIGHT WALL

- Glue B1 to glue track B1 next to decorated column.
- Glue wall and door drapes to stage floor B2, B3, B4, B5, B6, B7, B8.
- Glue B9 flap to centre wall back.
- Glue pelmet B10, B11 to wall, B12 to centre pelmet.
- Glue feathers B13 to corner openings.

STAGE LEFT WALL

- Glue C1 to glue track C1 next to decorated column.
- Glue wall to stage floor C2, C3, C4, C5, C6.
- Glue C7 flap to centre wall back.
- Glue pelmet C8, C9, to wall; C10 to centre pelmet.
- Glue feathers C11 to corner openings.

DAIS

- Glue to wall D1 and to stage floor D.

DANCERS

- Fold back flaps, glue along lines on the rostrum, dais, stage floor, on top of the small matching numbers.

CEILING DRAPERIES

- Glue to hanger along glue track.

CHANDELIER

- Glue chandelier E to back of ceiling draperies.

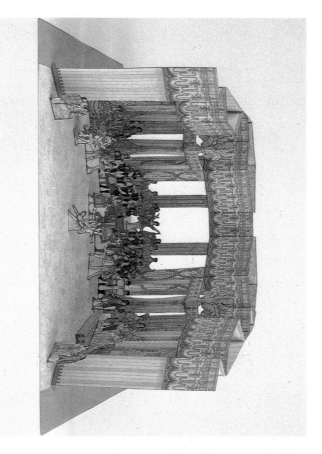

◀ STAGE RIGHT

STAGE LEFT ▶

DO NOT CUT OUT from this side

133

The Sleeping Beauty **Act 4** Stage floor   CUT OUT from this side

A 25
A 24
A 21
A 20

A 10

A9

C A
10 26

A19 B12 B12

D

D1

B3

22

5

4

3

1

12

X

A

V

A15

A14

A16

A13

A12

A17

B4

A3

A7 A8

A1

A2

A5 A6

2

5

1

4

3

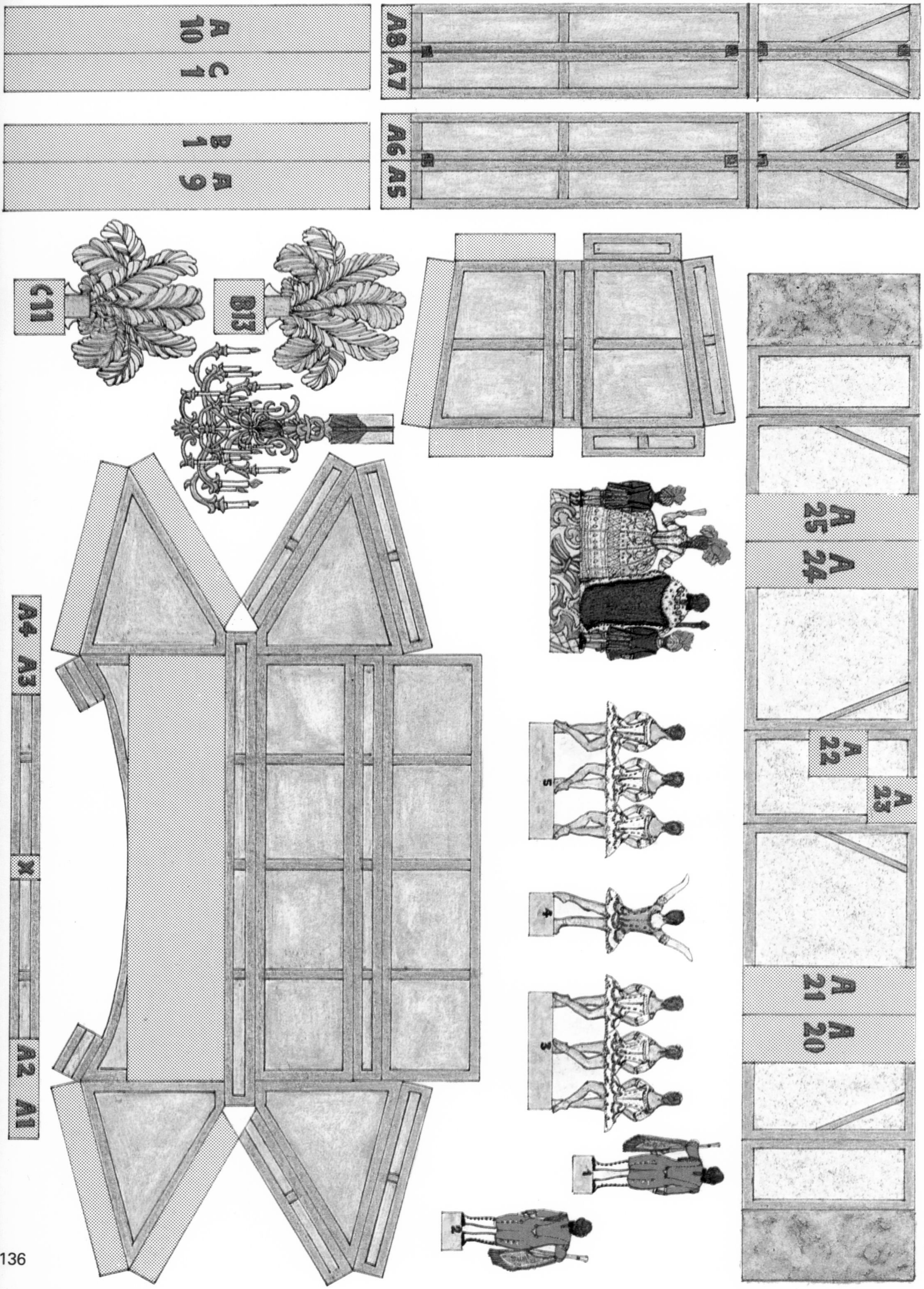
A 10
C 1
B 1
A 9
A8 A7
A6 A5
C11
B13
A 25
A 24
A 22
A 23
A 21
A 20
A4 A3
X
A2 A1
5
4
3
1
2

DO NOT CUT OUT from this side

CUT OUT from this side Act 4 Stage right: pelmet, stage centre: wall, stage left: pelmet

12

14

16

11

13

7

8

B11

C9

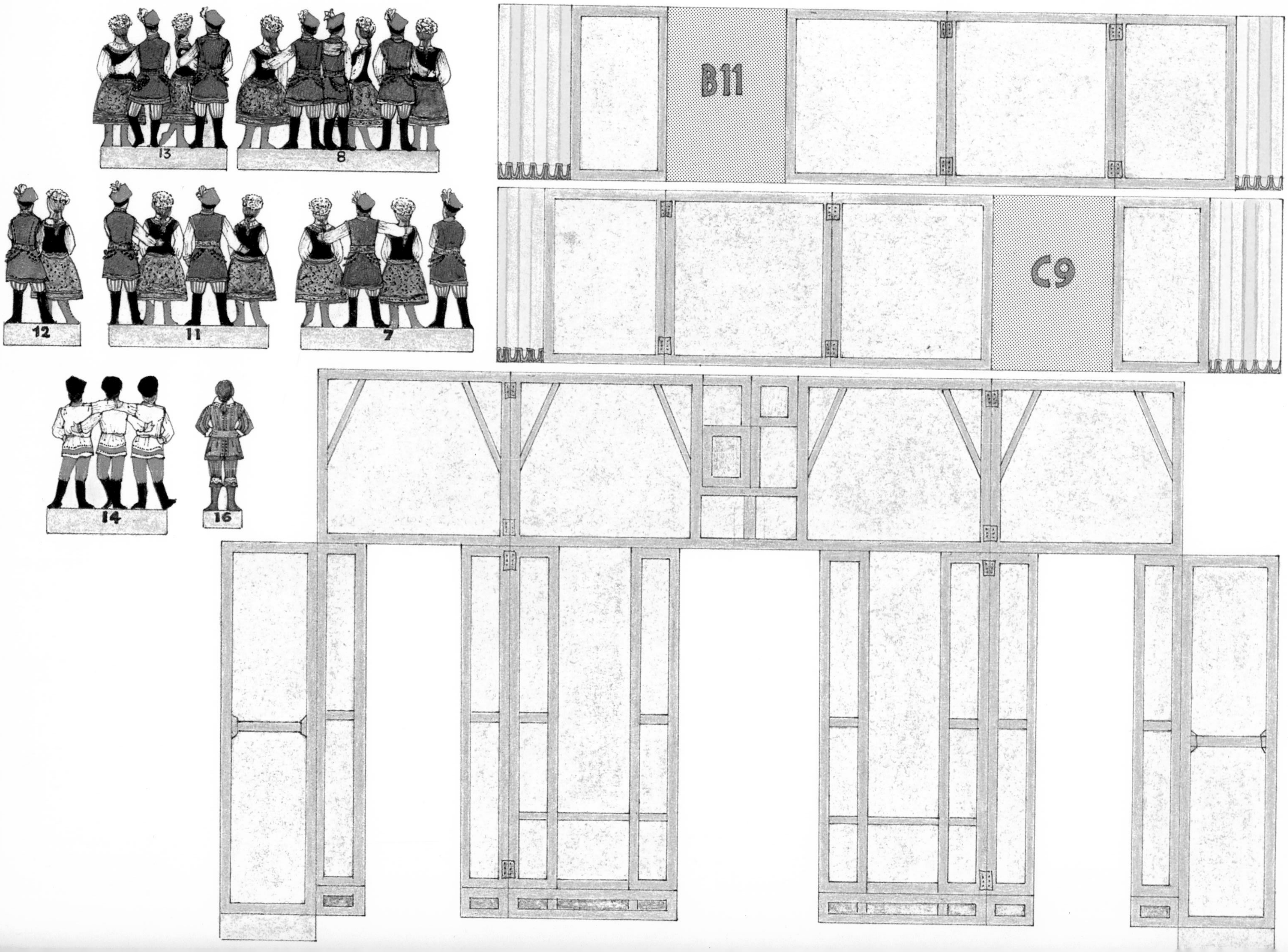

C7
C9
C8
C11
D1
C4
C5
C6
C2
C3

B10
B11
B9
B13
B8
B7
B6
B5
B4
B3
B2

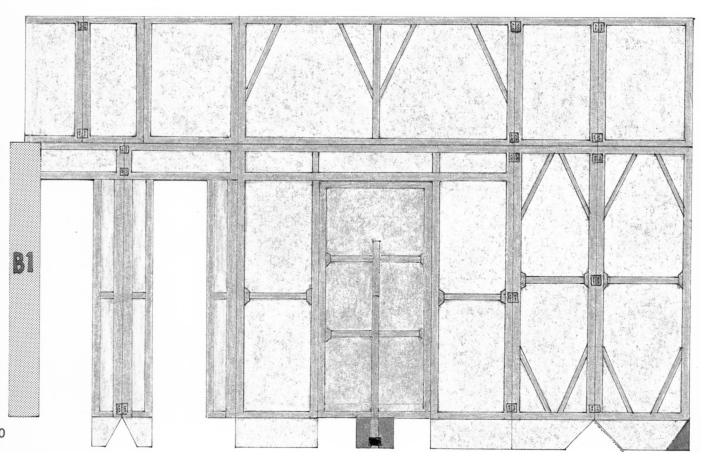

B1

DO NOT CUT OUT from this side

CUT OUT from this side **Act 4** Ceiling draperies

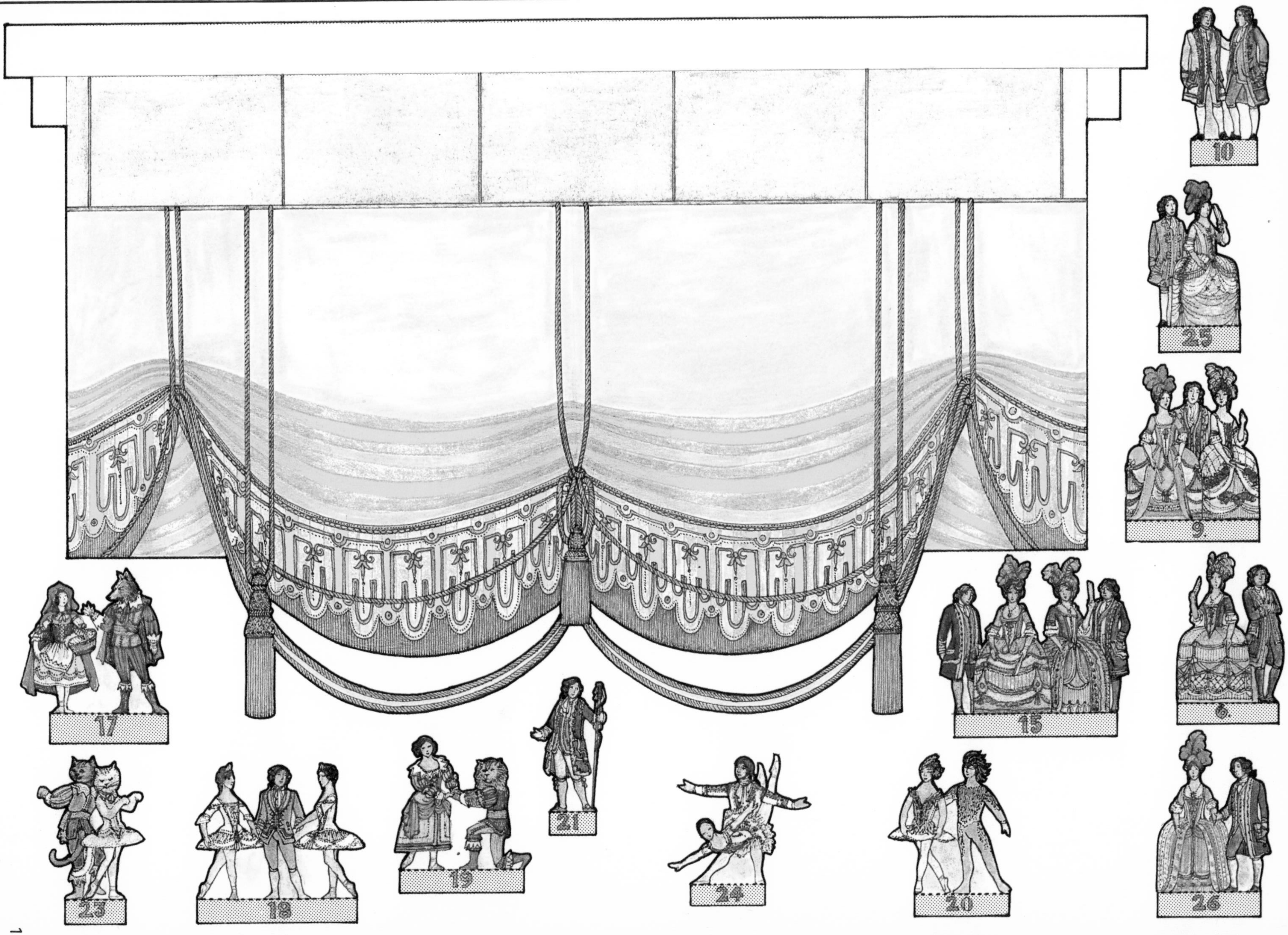

THE SLEEPING BEAUTY (ACT 4), CEILING DRAPERIES: GRID SLOT 4

DO NOT CUT OUT from this side